# SAS

## IN ACTION

PARRAGON

# SAS
## IN ACTION

**CHRIS CHANT**

First published in Great Britain in 1997 by
Parragon
13 Whiteladies Road
Clifton
Bristol
BS8 1PB

This paperback edition published in 1998

**ISBN 0-75252-584-0**

Conceived, designed and produced by
Brown Packaging Books Ltd
Bradley's Close
74-77 White Lion Street
London N1 9PF

Design: WDA

Printed in Italy

**Picture Acknowledgements**
*Military Picture Library:* 11, 24, 34, 71, 74, 85, 88,
89, 91, 94
*Photo Press:* 2-3, 6, 9, 10, 44, 49, 54, 67, 77, 78,
79, 90, 91, 92
*Soldier Magazine:* 31, 56, 70
*TRH Pictures:* 7, 8, 12, 13, 14, 15, 16, 19 (both),
20, 21, 22, 23, 25 (both), 26 (both), 28, 29 (both),
30 (both), 33, 35, 36, 38 (both), 40, 41, 42 (both),
43 (both), 45, 46, 47, 48, 50, 51, 52, 53, 55 (both),
57, 59, 60 (both), 61, 62 (both), 64, 65, 66, 68
(both), 72, 73 (both), 74, 75, 76, 80, 81 (both), 83,
84, 85, 86, 87, 93, 95 (both)

**Artwork Acknowledgements**
*Malcolm McGregor:* 17, 18, 21, 27, 34, 37, 39, 40, 63
*Steve Seymour:* 11, 59, 82

# CONTENTS

# CHAPTER 1

# SELECTION AND TRAINING

**Famed for its fitness and elite fighting skills, the SAS uses a rigorous selection and training procedure to turn a soldier of the British Army into a trooper of the SAS – only the best will do.**

As a unit with the highest standards of physical fitness and an exacting military role, Britain's Special Air Service (SAS) Regiment only accepts those men who have passed its gruelling selection and training procedures. This is designed specifically for the task of eliminating not only the unsuitable but also the marginally suitable, so that those who are left possess the physical and mental qualities that experience has taught to be essential for success on operations: physical strength and endurance, mental toughness and resilience, a moral character that includes

*ABOVE: A lone figure tramps wearily across Pen-y-Fan, the highest peak in the Brecon Beacons. The culmination of SAS Selection is the 'Fan Dance', a 60km (37-mile) march over the highest peaks in the Brecons, which must be completed in under 20 hours.*

*LEFT: Potential SAS recruits make a static-line parachute jump during their parachute training course at RAF Brize Norton, Oxon.*

determination and self-reliance, and the intelligence to allow a man to work his way through a problem however dire the situation.

The Regiment considers only those men who have volunteered for service with the SAS after a period of enlistment with a regular unit of the British Army and, to a lesser extent, the Royal Air Force, and this fact has the immediate advantage of eliminating what would otherwise be a spate of civilian volunteers thinking that the SAS provided the type of military 'glamour' sometimes attributed in the past and, among the more impressionable, even in the present to organisations such as the French Foreign Legion or even mercenary organisations.

This rule about accepting only men currently serving with the British forces is entirely inflexible. It means that the SAS is able to draw its strength from men in their mid- to late 20s who possess a strong measure of physical and mental maturity, are already well versed in the basic

military skills, and who have at least three years and three months of service left from the time they pass SAS Selection Training.

*ABOVE: Silent killing skills are an essential part of being an SAS soldier, and involve being able to stalk the target silently. These techniques are taught after recruits have passed Continuation.*

### SELECTION TRAINING

This course is run twice a year – once in the summer and once in the winter. After volunteering and being initially assessed for suitability, each man must wait until he is called to fill a vacancy in the Selection Training programme. The attributes required of a candidate include motivation, determination, initiative, self-discipline, compatibility within small groups undertaking isolated and long-endurance missions, the ability to assimilate a wide range of skills, and the flexibility of mind that allows rapid and effective lateral thinking. It is thought that initial assessment on the basis of these requirements eliminates 90 per cent of candidates before the Selection Training programme.

Knowing what is ahead in terms of physical and mental effort, most soldiers spend as much time and effort as possible in the preparation of body and mind before the Selection Training programme.

The programme lasts four weeks and is operated by the Training Wing of 22 SAS at Stirling Lines, the SAS's UK base at Hereford. The programme is based on that designed in 1953 by Major John Woodhouse, an SAS veteran of the Malayan Emergency (see Chapter 3). The programme starts with a build-up period, which lasts for two weeks in the case of officers and three weeks for the men of other ranks. Although each volunteer must have been certified fit by his own regimental medical officer, the SAS feels that at this early stage it is both sensible and fair to give each man a chance to come up to the Regiment's physical requirements. During the first week, therefore, volunteers start with a series of road runs that increase in length over the week. Each volunteer must also be able to demonstrate that he is capable of passing the standard Battle Fitness Test in the time allotted for infantrymen and paratroops. Regarded as a minimum standard, however, this is another way to weed out unsuitable volunteers, before the remainder are sent on a number of timed cross-country marches over the Black Mountains and the Brecon Beacons of South Wales. This is difficult country for movement and subject to rapid changes in weather conditions. The object of this stage of the programme is not only to assess the candidates' physical condition and resilience, but also to test their capabilities in the wholly essential skills of map reading and navigation.

The men are separated from their original partners and assigned marching and map reading tasks with bergen packs increased in weight steadily from 11 to 25kg (24-55lb). Candidates must also complete the marching and map reading tasks within an unknown time limit set by the programme's controllers; the candidate must therefore push himself to the limit to ensure success. Candidates have to cope with additional factors such as rain, which will soak into the bergen and make it heavier, increasing the possibility of becoming lost – which may result in the need to jog for the rest of the way to make up time – and the likelihood of being stopped at check points to strip a foreign weapon or answer questions on topics such as a landmark he passed some time ago. At all times, a candidate's reactions as well as answers are monitored as part of the continuous assessment of his abilities as a potential SAS trooper.

It is an extremely intense programme: a typical day begins at 0400 hours and can end as late at 2230 hours or later with a briefing for the next day's exercise. The result is an accumulation of physical and mental fatigue as the course itself becomes more demanding. This is a deliberate policy to ensure that an individual has the ability to operate effectively under increasing pressure, and that only the best finally get through.

The staff of the Selection Training programme is maintain an air of deliberate neutrality, designed to assess the candidate's self motivation and ability to

## SAS VOLUNTEER QUALIFICATION AND SELECTION

To qualify for possible service with the SAS Regiment, the volunteer must be currently serving with a corps or regiment of the regular British Army, and must have at least three years and three months of service left from the date of selection for the SAS. Run by the Training Wing at Stirling Lines, the SAS Regiment's base in Hereford, the Selection programme is based on a four-week course comprising hill walking, marching, navigation, physical training and classroom exercises culminating in Test Week. This involves six hill-walking exercises with a personal weapon and a bergen weighing up to 25kg (55lb) and ends with the gruelling 60km (37-mile) Endurance March. Successful candidates then progress to the Continuation Training, Jungle Training, and Parachute Course elements of post-Selection training that last a total of 24 weeks and end with the volunteer being 'badged' as a member of the SAS Regiment for progression to the advanced training element of his route towards full service with the Regiment.

*BELOW: SAS weapons skills stress firing assault rifles and machine guns in short, controlled bursts. Every round must be made to count when operating deep behind enemy lines.*

function as an individual, an asset much prized by the SAS. Although the Regiment utilises the four-man patrol as its basic unit, most of the world's other elite forces place a somewhat higher emphasis on the integration of the soldier's capabilities into the unit, either small or large. The SAS, however, emphasise individualism, which they believe allows a man to function more capably in extreme conditions.

### TEST WEEK AND THE 'LONG DRAG'

At the end of the two- or three-week build-up period, many of the candidates have been lost from the programme, some at their own request, as they appreciate their unsuitability for the unit, and others who have been "binned" by the programme-management team or returned to their original unit (RTU'd). A smaller number of candidates embark on the final stage of the Selection Training programme – Test Week.

Test Week is an intensive seven days of gruelling tests and assessments culminating in the 'Long Drag' or 'Fan Dance', which is a 60km (37-mile) land navigation exercise over the highest points in the Brecon Beacons (including Pen-y-fan, the highest peak, hence the nickname). The candidate embarks on this ordeal with his personal weapon and a 25kg (55lb) bergen, and is faced with the task of completing the course in

*BELOW: A static-line parachute drop from a C-130 Hercules transport aircraft. After they have won their 'wings' on static-line jumps, SAS soldiers go on to learn freefall parachuting.*

20 hours, regardless of weather conditions that are often vile and may be appalling, even in the summer. The nature and consequences of the 'Fan Dance' may be summarised by the results of one such march in the early part of 1992: of the 149 candidates who started, 61 failed to complete the course or parts of it in the allotted times, 59 pulled out, six were injured and eight were 'binned' by the instructor team, leaving a mere 15 men who were judged suitable for the next phase of SAS training, which is deemed applicable only to the men who have now proved their combination of physical endurance and mental determination.

### FIELDCRAFT AND THE FOUR-MAN PATROL

Once he has successfully completed the 'Fan Dance', the candidate for SAS membership moves forward to the Continuation Training programme, which lasts 14 weeks and is designed to provide candidates with the basic skills demanded of SAS troopers. The skills are the minimum requirement for any new trooper, to enable him to be integrated successfully into a four-man patrol – the smallest of the SAS's operational units. Standard operating procedures (SOPs), as they are referred to, include movement through hostile territory, the arcs of fire of each patrol member, and contact drills. Each student also receives training in the art of signalling, which is vital to the task of four-man patrols: all students must achieve the British Army's Regimental Signaller standard, which includes the ability to send and receive Morse code at the mini-

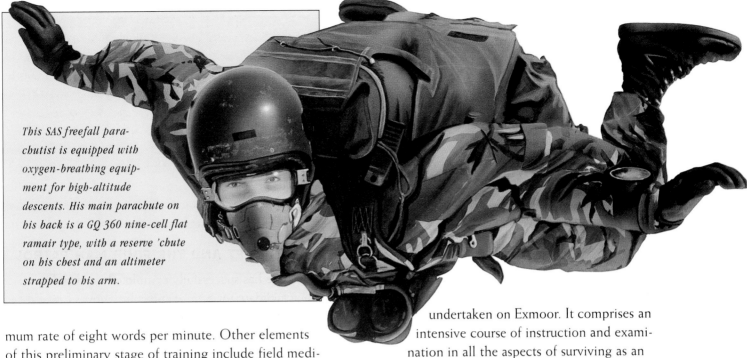

*This SAS freefall para-chutist is equipped with oxygen-breathing equip-ment for high-altitude descents. His main parachute on his back is a GQ 360 nine-cell flat ramair type, with a reserve 'chute on his chest and an altimeter strapped to his arm.*

mum rate of eight words per minute. Other elements of this preliminary stage of training include field medi-cine, basic demolition skills and languages.

Within the four-man patrol each trooper is assigned a specific role. When moving in file, for example, the leading man covers the area to the front of the patrol in the arc between 10 and two o'clock, the man behind him (usually the patrol commander) covers the arc between six and 10 o'clock or between two to six o'clock, the third man covers the opposite arc to the man in front, and the fourth man, 'tail end Charlie', covers the rear of the patrol. The small size of the four-man patrol places many demands on the individ-ual – SOP skills must become second nature to the candidate to ensure the survival of it's members. Failure to cover an assigned arc, could be a fatal mis-take, but just as important are the basics of fieldcraft – target reconnaissance, weapons training, and ground control of artillery fire and aircraft fire.

### COMBAT AND SURVIVAL TRAINING

To progress to the next stage of Continuation Training the candidate must pass the test in basic fieldcraft The object, however, is not merely to pass, but to excel, and the training staff will rapidly 'bin' any candidate who is merely adequate. There are numerous initiative tests along the way, each designed to assess the candi-date's self reliance, his ability to think for himself, and also to spur him on to greater efforts.

With these fundamental skills taken on board as part of his mental set, the candidate progresses to the part of next part of Continuation training – Combat and Survival techniques. This lasts for three weeks and is

undertaken on Exmoor. It comprises an intensive course of instruction and exami-nation in all the aspects of surviving as an effective soldier in a hostile environment. The basic elements of the survival training programme include shelter building, finding food and water, laying traps for small game, and making fire.

### SABRE SQUADRON ORGANISATION

The SAS Regiment is divided into four opera-tional Sabre squadrons: A, B, D and G Squadrons, with R Squadron in reserve. Each of these squadrons has 64 men under the command of a major, and is divided into four 16-man troops each com-manded by a captain. Each of these troops in turn has its own speciality: the Boat Troop is used for all aspects of amphibious warfare; the Mobility Troops for all aspects of land mobility by Land Rover, fast-attack vehicle and motorcycle; the Air Troop deals with all aspects of freefall parachuting; and the Mountain Troop for all aspects of mountaineering and winter warfare. Each troop is further divided into four four-man patrols, each led by a corporal, and the fighting patrol is the SAS Regiment's basic tactical unit. Rotation of men through the troops helps to ensure a wide level of cross-discipline training and experience.

*ABOVE: Signalling skills are taught to potential SAS recruits during Continuation Training. The minimum standard is being able to transmit and receive Morse at a rate of eight words a minute.*

The final week of the Combat and Survival course ends with an Escape and Evasion exercise, in which the candidate has to avoid capture by an 'enemy' force, which is generally a battalion of locally based infantry. At the end of the exercise all those who have evaded capture must 'surrender' themselves at a 'compromised rendezvous point', from where they are moved to an interrogation centre, undergo perhaps the most mentally gruelling part of an SAS soldiers' training, the 24-hour Resistance-to-Interrogation exercise. Throughout this exercise, the candidate is subjected to extremes of both mental and physical stress, through, for example, sleep deprivation, intensive questioning and humiliation. All aspects of the course are designed to make men yield information beyond the permitted maximum of name, number, rank and date of birth. This is a particularly difficult aspect of the candidate's training and, as with every other part of the programme, any man who fails the test is summarily rejected for further training and RTU'd. Those who pass can congratulate themselves on having completed Continuation Training.

The survivors are then moved to a very different environment for a period of intensive tuition in jungle survival and warfare. Jungle training lasts between four and six weeks and is undertaken in the Far East, most commonly Brunei. The object of the course is to teach the candidate basic jungle survival techniques – navigation in the dark, dense jungle, identifying edible flora and fauna, building concealed hides, for example. The course ends with an exercise: a four-man patrol is given a specific task that is designed to test to the limit all the skills the candidates have been taught in the preceding weeks. Once again, the course must be successfully completed if the student is to avoid being RTU'd and go forward to static-line parachute training at No 1 Parachute Training School, based at RAF Brize Norton in Oxfordshire.

Following the Jungle Training programme, potential officers are required to undergo a series of written tests, all of which are intended to provide the assessment team with an insight into the candidate's ability to make the right command decisions under severe stress. The officer candidate typically gets only 15 hours of sleep in a five-day period, and his plans and thinking are constantly criticised.

## OFFICERS' WEEK

The week starts with an initial exercise, in which the candidate firstly introduces himself, his background and his ambitions to an audience and then completes a number of problem-solving exercises where the candidate must offer deductions and solutions as well as answering questions. Each candidate is also given a written problem every day and a practical task that must be completed every night.

---

### STIRLING LINES

The base occupied by the SAS Regiment in Hereford since 1960 was originally called Bradbury Lines. By the early 1980s, however, the buildings were somewhat dilapidated, and as part a program of repair and refurbishment, a new barracks block was constructed and completed. The block was completed in 1984, and the base was renamed Stirling Lines in honour of the regiment's founder, David Stirling. Stirling Lines is occupied by 22 SAS Regiment under the command of a lieutenant-colonel, and the elements of the Regiment at this base are the Training Wing, Counter Revolutionary Warfare Wing, Operations Research Wing, Demolitions Wing, Operations Planning & Intelligence (known as 'the Kremlin'), 264 SAS Signals Squadron on detachment from the Royal Corps of Signals, four Sabre Squadrons as the Regiment's fighting squadrons, and R Squadron, the regimental reserve.

The attributes demanded of an SAS officer include strong motivation and full commitment, a forceful personality and complete integrity, the ability to think both logically and laterally, organisational skill, adaptability, and an overall measure of confidence including decisiveness, intelligence and common sense. All these factors, as well as the results of the Officers' Week testing, are taken into account in the final assessment of officer candidates.

## STATIC-LINE PARACHUTING

For all potential SAS recruits, the last stage of training is the Static-Line Parachute Training course. This four-week course involves eight jumps including one from a static (tethered) balloon, one at night and one at low level under operational conditions.

It is only on the successful completion of this stage that the candidate is finally awarded his 'Sabre' wings and, on return to Hereford, finally accepted as a 'badged' member of the SAS entitled to wear the Regiment's beige beret and winged dagger badge.

Arduous though they are, the Selection and Continuation programmes are designed to ensure that the quality of soldiers the SAS Regiment receives are up to it's exacting standards. In the following 12 months of probationary service, the SAS trooper joins a four-man patrol. It is here that the real training effort is undertaken. The new trooper learns his specialised patrol skill (medicine, demolition, communication or language) as well as the particular skills of the troop to which he has been assigned. Each of the SAS's four Sabre Squadron have four 16-man troops, and each of these specialises in a particular aspect of the Regiment's operational requirements: each squadron includes one Mountain Troop, one Boat Troop, one Mobility Troop and one Air Troop.

The important thing at this stage is that the new trooper gains a mastery of his particular patrol skill, but it is not unusual for troopers to gain a second and even a third skill during their service with the Regiment – it can never be said that there exists any such animal as a 'fully trained SAS trooper'. During operations, this multi-skill capability gives an the regiment an enormous tactical advantage, as it enables a small patrol to function even after losing one of it's specialists.

In addition to its training in patrol and troop skills, each Sabre Squadron is given specialised training in counter-revolutionary warfare. The squadrons are rotated through the Counter Revolutionary Warfare (CRW) Wing's facility at the Regiment's Hereford base for thorough training in all aspects of counter-terrorism and hostage-rescue. At any time there is always one squadron on 24-hour standby for counter-terrorism and/or hostage-rescue situations.

*BELOW: Two combat swimmers emerge from the surf during an amphibious exercise. Each SAS Sabre Squadron has a 16-man Boat Troop, which specialises in all aspects of maritime and subaqua combat and infiltration techniques.*

# CHAPTER 2

# WORLD WAR II

**The SAS was born in the North African campaign of World War II, then fought through Italy and Northwest Europe, harassing the enemy with a mix of demolition attacks and roving disruption work.**

The origins of the Special Air Service Regiment can be found in North Africa during the earlier part of World War II. Lieutenant-Colonel David Stirling succeeded in bluffing his way to an interview with Major General Neil Ritchie, the deputy commander-in-chief in the Middle East and North Africa, from who he gained authorisation to form a reconnaissance and demolition unit designed to

*ABOVE: An Afrika Korps soldier keeps watch in North Africa in 1942. Despite such precautions, SAS patrols were able to infiltrate Axis territory to raid airfields and depots in 1942-43.*

*LEFT: An SAS Jeep machine gunner in North Africa, 1942. Each vehicle was armed with at least three machine guns for the purposes of raiding enemy targets. Note the twin Vickers 'K' guns behind him.*

operate behind the German and Italian lines. The unit came into existence in July 1941 and was known as L Detachment, Special Air Service Brigade. 17 November 1941 is regarded as the 'birthday' of the SAS, however, as this was the date of the unit's first raid. L Detachment did not officially become 1 SAS until October 1942.

## EARLY MISSIONS

The unit's first operation was an attack on two Axis airfields in the area of Gazala and Tmimi, as part of Operation 'Crusader'. 'Crusader' was General Claude Auchinleck's strategy to drive the German and Italian forces out of Cyrenaica on the western frontier of Egypt, where they posed a severe threat to Cairo and the Suez Canal. The 65 SAS troopers were dropped by parachute on the night of 16/17 November , but the mission was a total disaster as the men and their equipment were blown all over the drop zone by the high wind. Several men were injured when they landed, some of them badly, and as a consequence the mission had to be abandoned.

### RITE OF PASSAGE

It was a daunting setback, particularly as it occurred during the unit's first operational effort, but the SAS continued to train for attacks on airfields and vitally important depots behind Axis lines. Stirling had decided after the first mission that parachuting was not the right insertion method, and that the vehicles of the Long Range Desert Group (LRDG), another behind-the-lines reconnaissance and demolition outfit, would provide the best means of transport.

This change in operational procedure was immediately successful: in December 1941 the SAS launched attacks against the Axis airfields at Sirte, Agheila, Tamit, Nofilia and 'Marble Arch'. These actions resulted in the destruction of about 100 Axis aircraft, although the inherent dangers of this type of operation were revealed by the comparative failure of the Nofilia attack. On 26 December a unit under the com-

mand of Lieutenant 'Jock' Lewes succeeded in destroying only two aircraft at Nofilia, but Italian aircraft attacked the SAS convoy as it was withdrawing and killed Lewes.

The new year brought more success, vindicating Stirling's belief in the effectiveness of small-sized groups operating behind the lines. No two of these hit-and-run mission were exactly the same, but all shared a number of features in common. The trip to the operational area in the trucks of the LRDG was usually uneventful, but a constant watch had to be kept for Axis aircraft, which could swoop down and cause devastating damage if not detected early enough for the party to conceal itself or take cover.

The action that followed once a raiding party had reached its target was less glamourous and, wherever possible, less exciting than might be expected. It was just as important in World War II, as it is now, to infiltrate the target area undetected, lay the explosive charges, and then withdraw with as little fuss as possible: the last thing that any small unit operating deep

*BELOW: David Stirling, the founder of the SAS (far right) with one of his Jeep columns in North Africa, late 1942. Note the Jerry cans for fuel and water on the bonnets and sides of the vehicles.*

## OPERATIONAL BACKGROUND

The SAS was created in 1941 during World War II, and fought in the North African theatre (1940-43), the Italian theatre (1943-45) and the Northwest European theatre (1944-45). British, German and Italian troops in the North African theatre fought a series of see-sawing campaigns, although the inadequacy of Axis supply lines eventually proved to be the single most decisive factor. The Allies gained the upper hand late in 1942 at the Second Battle of El Alamein in the east at the same time as amphibious landing in the west involving American and British forces. The Allies then advanced from east and west, finally squeezing the Axis forces into surrender during May 1943 in Tunisia. Embarking for Italy, the Allies descended on Sicily and then the mainland of Italy, slowly fighting their way north toward Austria along the eastern and western sides of the central Apennine mountain range. The Northwest European campaign started in June 1944 with the Normandy landings, and then took the form of an Allied broad-front advance though France and into the Low Countries as well as western Germany, before the German armies were ground into final defeat in May 1945.

behind the enemy's lines wants is to attract attention, which will necessarily result in the arrival of substantially larger numbers of enemy troops who may be too late to prevent the unit achieving its objective but probably not too late to prevent its escape.

### DESERT RAIDS

Typical of the raids undertaken in the first part of 1942 was the raid on Berka Satellite airfield, part of the major Berka Main airfield complex near the North African coast, on 8 March 1942. Under the command of Captain 'Paddy' Mayne, the attacking party avoided the German sentries guarding the perimeter of the airfield and split into two groups. The charges they laid destroyed some 15 aircraft, to the complete bewilderment of the Germans. On 13 June both airfields were attacked, with Mayne again leading the attack on Berka Satellite. This time the Germans were more vigilant, for the attacking party was detected as it tried to infiltrate the airfield. They were forced to pull back without inflicting any damage. The other party was more successful and destroyed 11 aircraft.

The early success of the SAS parties meant that the Germans and Italians soon tightened security around

their airfields. Most raiding parties also feared that a successful attack would make it more difficult to rejoin their LRDG 'delivery service', as the now thoroughly alerted Axis forces would scour the area with light armour and aircraft. If the enemy succeeded in finding and either destroying or dispersing the LRDG truck group, or alternatively in preventing the link-up of the two groups, the men of the SAS party were then faced with the difficult and extremely arduous task of reaching their own lines by a long overland march through territory that was naturally hostile to man, as well as patrolled by the enemy.

In January 1943, Major 'Bill' Fraser led a successful attack on 'Marble Arch' airfield. Reaching the rendezvous point without knowing that the relevant LRDG patrol had been despatched to the wrong point, the SAS team waited in vain for its transport. When it became clear that the LRDG was not going to arrive, the men decided to walk the 320km (200 miles) back to base, The training programme devised by 'Jock' Lewes revealed its full value. One of the group, Private Byrne, describes the journey: 'We took turns to lead, every one of us setting a cracking pace, determined to match each other's resolution. Weary beyond belief, we kept tramping on, stamping our feet into the soft desert sand and lifting them up again like automata, every step an effort ... The sun burned into eyes from high overhead and was reflected up again from the sand. There was no escape from it and we longed for the luxury of sun glasses or a peaked cap. At dusk we dug holes in the sand, curled up in our

*North Africa, 1942. Lieutenant Edward McDonald, SAS, in typical desert attire. He wears an Arab shemagh on his head, leather gauntlets and Arab sandals. His weapons comprise Sykes-Fairbairn Commando dagger and Webley pistol.*

blankets and tried to sleep.' The fact that all the men of the party made it back to the British lines is testimony to the stamina that came increasingly to characterise the SAS soldier.

Mid-1942 witnessed a change in SAS battle tactics. Stirling's men adopted the American Willys Jeep, which despite their comparatively small size, were heavily armed (two 0.303in Vickers 'K' light machine guns mounted front and rear and often bolstered by a 0.5in Browning heavy machine gun) and well equipped for long-range operations in the North African desert. Together with water condensers, the vehicles carried sand mats, radio equipment, metal wheel channels and a mass of spare ammunition. The Jeeps were first used by the SAS during its attack on Bagoush airfield during 7 July 1942, with Stirling and Mayne among the officers involved. Three heavily armed Jeeps drove onto the airfield's runway and past the parked aircraft, riddling them with ball, tracer, and armour-piercing rounds. The airfield's garrison offered no opposition, and the SAS party destroyed 37 aircraft, some of them with explosive charges.

As the North African campaign drew to a close in the early summer of 1943, the two SAS regiments, now totalling some 600 men, seemed to be on the verge of disbanding. Senior staff however, appreciated that Stirling (who had been captured in January 1943) had brought into existence an organisation that was

*Special Boat Squadron (SBS) officer, late 1943. His uniform consists of khaki denim overalls, puttees and civilian suede boots, which could withstand rough treatment. His beige beret and Winged Dagger badge indicates he was originally in the SAS.*

capable of undertaking offensive operations in any theatre rather than just the desert. The SAS was thus well suited to a role in the Allies' next strategic moves: the invasion of Sicily in July 1943 and the leap onto the Italian mainland in September of the same year.

During Operation 'Husky', the codename for the invasion of Sicily , the Special Raiding Squadron (1 SAS with a temporary change of name) came under the command of the British XIII Corps, and was entrusted with the task of capturing the gun battery on Capo Murro di Porco after an amphibious landing. The raid was undertaken on 10 July 1943. Rough seas made it difficult for the men to load into their landing craft, and on arrival the 40 men of the attacking party climbed to the lighthouse but found it deserted.

## CLEARING ITALY

During the Sicilian campaign the SAS made its first acquaintance with a new type of combat: urban fighting. Once again exhaustive training combined with general professionalism provided the answer: for example, when moving along a street, an SAS section would split into two with the group on one side of the street covering the group opposite The rear man of each group walked backwards to provide protection against attack from the rear. On discovery of an occupied building, a shower of grenades would be thrown through the windows followed by a rapid entry through the smashed-down door with all weapons firing. It was an unpopular, nasty form of fighting, but the SAS proved itself adept in the task.

A different tactic was used to clear Bagnara on the 'toe' of the Italian mainland at the beginning of September 1943. There, the SAS used vineyards as cover for longer-range fire with their Bren light machine guns and Vickers heavy machine guns. Conservation of ammunition was important, and the SAS achieved its tasks with the minimum expenditure of bullets and grenades by holding back until a definite target was observed.

From the earliest days, the SAS attached great importance to thorough and exhaustive weapons training. Stirling always emphasised the need for close familiarity with the weapons of the Axis forces as well as British and American weapons. This was particularly important for men who were to operate behind enemy lines. In fact, many SAS soldiers preferred to use captured weapons. The German 9mm MP40 submachine, for example, gun gained a good reputation among his men for its compactness.

## SIR DAVID STIRLING

In 1940 Stirling was a lieutenant in the Scots Guards and volunteered for No 8 Commando. Deployed to the Middle Eastern theatre as part of 'Layforce', Stirling participated in a number of unsuccessful commando raids on the North African coast, and became convinced that smaller units would be more effective. Hospitalised after a parachuting accident, Stirling completed detailed plans for his ideal raiding unit. He envisaged 200 men split into five-man units, which could achieve surprise and hit several targets on the same night, rather than using a large number of men to hit one target. Authorised to command the new L Detachment, Special Air Service Brigade in 1941, Stirling organised and trained his new unit, hand-picking his men, and improvising where necessary. He also impressed upon his superiors that the SAS could be used for attacks on targets whose destruction would aid the overall strategic plan. Captured in 1943, Stirling escaped four times, before being sent to Colditz, where he remained until 1945.

The SAS saw more action in the later stages of the Italian campaign, as Allied forces drove north towards the frontier with Austria. In this later period, the regiment was used for a number of amphibious operations along the coast of the Adriatic Sea and for operations in the German rear areas. Small raiding parties proved ability to undertake individually small but cumulatively effective attacks on targets such as railway lines and bridges, in an effort to hamper German lines of communication.

### BEHIND THE LINES, 1944-5

From June 1944, the SAS was heavily involved in the Allied campaign to liberate Northwest Europe from German occupation, and also played a highly active part in the final offensives into Germany that brought about the defeat of the Nazi war machine.

The operations of the SAS in France after the D-Day landings of 6 June 1944 can be divided into two main groups: the small-scale tactical support of General Sir Bernard Montgomery's 21st Army Group, and operations behind the German lines with local Maquis (resistance) groups. The object of the latter the disruption of German lines of communication, pre-

*BELOW: 2 SAS on parade after their hard-fought action at Termoli, Italy, October 1943. The officer (front row, left) is Major Sandy Scratchley. Note the insignia removed by wartime censors.*

venting the rapid movement of reinforcements between one part of the front and the other, and tying down sizeable numbers of troops in areas far from the main fighting. In the course of this combined effort, some 2000 SAS men were dropped behind enemy lines in France and the Low Countries in the four months following D-Day. Operating in uniform and able to fight with considerable mobility when provided with vehicles such as Jeeps dropped from aircraft, the men operated from more than 40 bases. For the loss of 330 of their own men, the SAS killed about 2000 Germans, wounded 7733, captured 4784 and negotiated the surrender of another 18,000, as well as destroying 700 vehicles and seven trains, derailing 33 trains and cutting railway lines on 164 occasions.

As is always the case in operations behind the enemy lines, SAS successes were directly proportional to the military skills of the personnel involved. A good example of this fact is provided by the story of Operation 'Kipling', which took place between 13 August and 26 September 1944 in the area west of Auxerre in northern part of central France. Under the command of Captain Derrick Harrison, the 107 men and 46 Jeeps involved in the operation were para-dropped by RAF aircraft in order to establish a forward base, from where they could roam into the German-held areas to the south of Orleans – the site of a scheduled Allied airborne operation. Harrison's

force established a safe base, into which additional men, vehicles and weapons were then delivered. The airborne operation was subsequently cancelled, and Harrison was ordered to forget his original instructions and start patrolling throughout his operational area with the object of killing and wounding as many Germans as possible and destroying or damaging their matériel.

### ICE COLD IN A FIREFIGHT

On 23 August, Harrison, at the head of a party in two Jeeps, decided to investigate smoke coming from the village of Les Ormes. As the SAS party approached, a fleeing civilian told him that the Germans were shooting up the entire village. The two Jeeps drove straight into the village square, shooting at German troops and vehicles as they did so. Harrison's Jeep stalled and the enemy started to fire back.

In these circumstances most men would have made a run for it or surrendered. Harrison, displaying the quick thinking and cool-headedness that was becoming a trademark of the SAS, opted for another course, however: 'I had grabbed my carbine and was now standing in the middle of the road firing at everything

*BELOW: Two SAS Jeeps of the 'Houndsworth' party behind enemy lines near Dijon, central France, early July 1944. Operation 'Houndsworth' was very successful, killing 200 German troops.*

## SABRE SQUADRON ORGANISATION

A legendary figure in the early days of the Special Air Service, Paddy Mayne was initially a member of No 11 (Scottish) Commando and was one of the first recruits to David Stirling's new desert unit. A superb leader and highly courageous, Mayne was involved in many raids against Axis airfields, personally destroying more than 100 Axis aircraft. Mayne believed that the SAS, rather than relying on the Long Range Desert Group, should have it own transport to reach targets, and this was the origin of the SAS's celebrated Jeep capability. In March 1943 Mayne was given command of the Special Raiding Squadron (the renamed 1 SAS), which he commanded through the Sicilian and Italian campaigns as a lieutenant-colonel. Mayne later led 1 SAS during the campaign in Northwest Europe.Examples of his personal courage abound. Typical is one incident on 9 April 1945 when Mayne almost single-handedly saved a column of Canadian armour from a concealed German rocket team.

that moved. Germans seemed to be firing from every doorway. I felt my reactions speed up to an incredible level. It was almost as if I could see individual bullets coming towards me as I ducked and weaved to avoid them. And all the time I was shooting from the hip, and shooting accurately'.

Despite an injury to his right arm, Harrison managed to reach the other Jeep, which made a speedy retreat from the village, leaving some 60 Germans dead and wounded, together with one truck and the two staff cars destroyed. For his bravery that day Harrison won a fully deserved Military Cross, but his actions also serve to highlight another important quality found in SAS soldiers: the ability not just to think, but to think constructively, even in an acutely difficult situation. Over the years, this quality had been instrumental in preserving the lives of many SAS men caught in very difficult situations.

In the early months of 1945 SAS units crossed into Germany. Here they found themselves in a very different type of situation, as it was no longer possible to

rely on the support of the local inhabitants. Long-range operations were generally eschewed in favour of more standard reconnaissance operations in front of conventional formations. Rather than driving deep in to the German rear areas, the men of the SAS fought just ahead of the advancing British and Canadian armies. Operating closer to the front, where the Germans could sensibly expect reconnaissance forces to be working, these Jeep-mounted SAS parties were more frequently caught in ambushes and therefore suffered proportionally higher losses than those endured in Italy and France.

The Jeeps used in this period reflected the fact that the SAS were operating in a more difficult situation: the entire front of the vehicle was covered with armour plate, there were semi-circular windscreens made of bulletproof glass to protect the driver and front gunner, and many of the vehicles were fitted with a wire-cutting device above the front bumper to prevent the decapitation of the team by wires strung across the road between trees or telegraph poles.

Germany surrendered at the beginning of May 1945, and after a short respite SAS soldiers arrived in Norway to supervise the surrender of the occupying German forces. With the surrender of Japan in August 1945 and the end of World War II, rapid demobilisation of the regiment began. The Special Air Service was officially disbanded in October 1945. It looked like the end, but a conflict on the other side of the world would soon require the particular talents of the SAS.

*This SAS officer of 1 SAS in 1945 wears a red beret instead of the normal beige variety. This is because the SAS Brigade was at the time a part of the 1st Airborne Corps. His 1937-pattern webbing pouches hold a compass and ammunition.*

# CHAPTER 3

# MALAYA AND BORNEO

## Disbanded in 1945, the SAS was resurrected in 1952 to meet a new challenge in the inhospitable jungles of Malaya, where the Regiment fought a war of cunning against an almost invisible enemy.

In the years following World War II, military analysts were concerned mainly with the emergence and development of the 'Cold War' between the USA and USSR. They focused on the role which the UK might possibly have to play if the 'Cold War' suddenly turned hot, in the event of a Soviet invasion of western Europe. The particular skills of the SAS were not utilised until the 'Emergency' in Malaya in June 1948.

The struggle between the British administration in Malaya and the Chinese-dominated Malayan Races Liberation Army (MRLA) lasted 12 years, but the fact

*ABOVE: During the campaign in Malaya in the 1950s, SAS patrols occasionally used the rivers which cut through the jungle, though rafts and small boats were very vulnerable to ambush from the banks.*

*LEFT: An SAS trooper on a village walkway in Borneo, early 1960s. He probably helped to build it as part of the Regiment's 'hearts and minds' effort to win over the locals – which succeeded.*

that the British finally defeated the Communist Terrorists (CTs), as the operatives of the MRLA came to be called, was in a large measure attributable to one man and the unit he created for his purpose.

Lieutenant-Colonel J.M. Calvert, often called 'Mad Mike', was in many respects a similar man to David Stirling: he had vision and was not afraid to consider unorthodox methods for the solution of problems. Calvert was a veteran of the 'Chindit' expeditions in Burma during World War II, and had ended the war in Europe in command of the SAS Brigade.

After initial British successes, the CTs had withdrawn into the jungles of Malaya, and from bases deep in this inhospitable terrain they launched attacks against almost defenceless British targets. It became clear to the authorities that long-term success against the CTs required the creation of a deep-penetration unit that could operate for extended periods in the jungle, tasked with seeking and destroying the bases used by the CTs.

Calvert submitted a report to General Sir John Harding, commander of the British land forces in the Far East, which described how to establish a specialised counter-insurgency unit able to live, move and fight the guerrillas effectively in the jungle.

### THE MALAYAN SCOUTS

In 1950 Calvert formed the Malayan Scouts. As well as a jungle warfare training centre based at Johore, the unit possessed an invaluable intelligence section under the command of Major John Woodhouse. The new unit launched a programme of three- and four-man patrols, which roved deep into the jungle for extended periods. Ambushes were laid, intelligence reports were compiled, and initial contacts were made with the Aboriginal peoples who had been pushed back into the interior of the Malay peninsula by successive waves of invaders. The Scouts rapidly became very successful. Their first operational area was the Ipoh region on the northern edge of the Cameron Highlands, but by June 1951 the Scouts were making their presence felt farther south in Johore province. In November of the year Calvert was invalided home,

## OPERATIONAL BACKGROUND

In an effort to meet the nationalist aspirations of the Malayan peoples after World War II, the British decided in 1948 to set up the Malay Federation, but this was unpopular with the Chinese minority as its gave political preponderance to the Malay majority. The communist element in this Chinese population formed the Malayan Races Liberation Army to wage a campaign of terror designed to force the British out of Malaya and end the Malay Federation. This heralded the start of the 'Emergency', which was to last to the late 1950s. The MRLA was combated initially by the Malayan Scouts, and, from 1952, by the SAS. During the Borneo 'Confrontation' of 1963-66, the SAS played a similar role, although in this instance against Indonesian troops. Indonesia tried to prevent the incorporation of the British possessions in Borneo into the enlarged Malaysian Federation. Intimidated by the size of the Federation, Indonesia wanted to seize Borneo, but was prevented from doing so by British troops, among them, the SAS.

and replaced by Lieutenant-Colonel John Sloane. The success of the Malayan Scouts continued, and in February 1952 the unit moved to the Belum valley, situated in the Kelantan province of northeast Malaya on the frontier with Thailand. It was here that the Scouts first used the 'tree jumping' technique for the delivery of patrols into thick jungle. The men parachuted into the jungle canopy, and then used long ropes to lower themselves to the ground.

The continued success of the Malayan Scouts was largely responsible for the re-creation, in 1952, of the Special Air Service regiment. The Scouts became the core of an SAS unit originally composed of a headquarters and four squadrons. The new organisation was made up of troops from the regimental base established by Woodhouse at the Airborne Forces Depot in Aldershot, during the autumn of 1952.

It should be noted that Calvert believed that direct military action was only one of the tools that could be employed against the CTs. He also wanted to win over the Aboriginal peoples as a means of denying the

*LEFT: In Malaya, the SAS were involved in mounting long-range patrols into the dense jungle, in order to root out communist terrorists. Some patrols lasted over three months, but the Regiment succeeded by 'taking the war to the enemy.'*

CTs the benefit of indigenous support. Calvert was also able to ensure that his patrols had accurate intelligence about the location and numerical strength of the MRLA in any given area. The Malayan conflict saw the beginning of the famous 'hearts and minds' policy that is now an intrinsic part of the SAS's operational philosophy.

## JUNGLE FIGHTING

Living and fighting in the Malayan jungle was an unpleasant and difficult experience. Much of the area was covered with dense stands of bamboo which made progress slow and excruciating. Often the only way to proceed was through the laborious use of a machete, whose cutting sound was a constant source of anxiety unless the presence of a troop of screaming monkeys covered it. Movement through swamps was equally slow and noisy, at a rate of perhaps 200m (660ft) per hour, and the men also had to contend with leeches. Movement through primary jungle was quieter and more rapid, as there was little that grew on the jungle floor. Here however, the soldiers had to avoid human and/or animal tracks, as these were often the sites of terrorist ambushes or booby traps.

Operating and fighting in the jungle needed great patience, nerves of steel, great physical strength and mental stamina. The floor of the jungle, under the all-covering canopy, was dark, humid and perpetually

*ABOVE: SAS parachutists check their equipment prior to boarding transport aircraft to take part in Operation 'Termite' in July 1954. This mission cleared the CTs out of Perak province.*

*BELOW: Tree jumping, a tactic used by the SAS in Malaya. Troopers were dropped by parachute and landed on the thick jungle canopy. However, after a number of fatalities it was scrapped.*

## MICHAEL CALVERT

A major figure in the rebirth of the SAS after World War II, Michael Calvert joined the Royal Engineers in 1933. Having worked in Military Intelligence Research and trained commandos, Calvert was next posted to Burma, where he joined the Chindits, operating deep behind Japanese lines.

Returning to Europe, Calvert became commander of the SAS Brigade in March 1944, a position he held until the unit was disbanded. In 1950, Calvert formed the Malayan Scouts, who were recruited from British military personnel in the Far East (especially former members of the SOE, Force 136 and Ferret Force), a force of Rhodesians, and 21 SAS Regiment, a territorial unit organising a detachment for service in Korea. Calvert also designed the operational procedure: 14-man units would be despatched into the jungle to establish a base from which small patrols of three to four men could gather intelligence, spring ambushes and destroy enemy bases. In 1952, the Malayan Scouts became 22 SAS Regiment.

BELOW: *A Malayan Scouts patrol in the Ipoh area of Malaya in November 1950. The brainchild of Mike Calvert, the Scouts operated in small-sized teams against the CTs.*

soaked by either sweat or rain. The men had to remain alert for an ambush or booby trap and the Malayan wildlife – from elephants, tigers, snakes, and water buffalo, to mosquitoes and hornets – could be very dangerous when startled. Even so, most SAS soldiers did not find the jungle threatening, for the floor was generally open, the temperature bearable, and in more mountainous areas there were many streams, little rivers and small lakes. There were frequent breaks, because of the combined weight of the men's 27kg (60lb) bergens and their individual weapons.

### SWAMP SKILLS

The jungle could be regarded with equanimity, but the same could not be said of the swamp regions, in particular Selangor province in the southwest of central Malaya. The predominant feature in this area is dense mangrove swamp, making progress slow and very laborious. The water is anything up to 1m (3ft) deep, and the standard method of progress employed by SAS troopers was across the roots of the tightly packed mangrove trees. Any slip or stumble would pitch the unfortunate man up to his waist in thick, black mud, from which it was notoriously difficult extricate oneself. Another problem to contend with were the countless tiger leeches that lurk in the swamp, whose bite, prior to the extraction of blood, is a painful distraction.

As the men of the SAS developed their skills in jungle warfare, new tactics were devised. 'Tree jumping' was a parachute technique pioneered by the SAS. As most CT camps were located deep in the jungle, it

took foot patrols a long time to reach them and therefore gave the enemy a good opportunity to escape. The decision was taken to drop men by parachute onto the thick jungle canopy from where they would use ropes to descend to the ground. The first operational jump was carried out in February 1952 near the Thai border by a detachment of 54 men. Their role was to act as a blocking force, in an operation that involved Gurkhas, Royal Marines, Malay Police and more SAS soldiers on the ground. None of the men deployed by parachute was injured, and the tactic was reckoned a great success. Parachuting into thick trees was in fact extremely hazardous, as confirmed during subsequent operations. There were a number of serious injuries: during Operation 'Sword,' in January 1954, three SAS soldiers died during a 'tree-jump' into the jungle canopy .

## MALAYAN VICTORY

By 1956 22 SAS numbered some 560 men, divided between the regimental headquarters and A, B, C, D, New Zealand and Parachute Squadrons. Notable operations in this period include the 14-week operation, commencing in April 1956, which involved the New Zealand Squadron in Perak and Kelantan provinces. The operation resulted in the destruction of the Asa (Aborigine) Organisation and the death of Ah Ming, its infamous leader. In May of that year, B Squadron began another 14-week-long operation. After a detailed search, they found and destroyed a large food crop on which large numbers of CTs relied. In this way the SAS harassed the CTs, and they were slowly worn down by shortages of food and weapons.

By 1958 the conflict in Malaya had almost been won. The last significant SAS operation in the 'Emergency' was undertaken by D Squadron under the command of Major H. Thompson. They moved into the swamp region near Telok Anson in the coastal part of Perak province with the object of finding and then either capturing or destroy-

ing the two terrorist groups under the leadership of Ah Hoi, nicknamed 'the Baby Killer'. It took no less than 10 days to establish a cordon around the area, which was then progressively tightened. As a result, 10 CTs including Ah Hoi surrendered – small-scale stuff by the standards of modern warfare, but it demonstrates effectively the tenacity, endurance and patrol skills of the SAS.

The SAS played a significant part, altogether greater than might have been imagined considering its comparatively small numerical strength, in the British victory against the CTs. In the jungle the SAS had won the 'hearts and minds' of the Aboriginal peoples and had made this type of terrain a thoroughly unsafe place for the CTs. Both the Malayan Scouts and the SAS showed convincingly that British troops, if they had the right physical and mental qualities and were correctly trained, could operate effectively in the jungle for long periods, and in the process take the war to the opposition.

By 1958, however, the SAS Regiment had once again fallen victim to 'downsizing'. In 1957, the unit found itself reduced to a headquarters and just two squadrons. In the following year, following protestations from officers such as General Sir Gerald Templar (the commander of the British forces throughout much of the Malayan 'Emergency'), wiser thoughts prevailed. The SAS was cut back in size, but it had a secure future as the most important repository within the British Army for the development and implementation of special fighting skills.

By the time the confrontation in Borneo had commenced in 1963, the SAS's drills

*An SAS trooper in Malaya, 1960. Armed with an Australian Owen submachine gun, distinguished by its top-mounted magazine, he wears a jungle-green drill uniform and canvas and rubber boots. Note the Malayan Command flash on his left shoulder.*

and procedures had been updated and refined. Helicopters were used for the insertion and extraction of troops on jungle operations, and for the supply, reinforcement and medical support of patrols.

By 1960 the SAS Regiment had the benefits of its own base in the UK and, as a result of the earlier efforts of Colonel Woodhouse, it could also boast an excellent Selection and Training programme that quickly and efficiently weeded out unsuitable candidates. The SAS Regiment was now truly one of the world's elite units.

### BORNEO 1963-66

When the British Government agreed to grant independence to Brunei, Malaya, Sabah, Sarawak and Singapore (collectively known as the Federation of Malaysia), it came into conflict with the territorial ambitions of President Sukarno of Indonesia. He regarded the potentially oil-rich British possessions of Brunei, Sabah and Sarawak on the northwestern side of the island of Borneo as prizes that could be absorbed into Indonesia, which already controlled three-quarters of Borneo as the province of Kalimantan.

Sukarno tried, through various means, to prevent the establishment of Malaysia. In December 1962 anti-Malaysian elements launched a rebellion in Brunei, which, although rapidly quelled by British troops, provided Sukarno with a pretext of 'democratic' forces

### JOHN WOODHOUSE

This exceptional officer is rightly regarded as one of the fathers of the modern SAS. He joined the British Army during 1941 as a private and remained in service after World War II. Having risen to the rank of major, Woodhouse was one of the earlier members of the Malayan Scouts, and was involved in the unit's reorganisation and helped to hone its jungle fighting skills. He demanded the highest levels of professionalism, physical fitness and discipline from the officers and men under his command, and repeated these demands when he returned to the UK in the summer of 1952 to organise recruitment procedures. The course he created became the basis of the current Selection and Continuation Training programmes. By 1962 this exceptionally fine leader of men was commanding 22 SAS in Borneo. Woodhouse continued to use the SAS with flair and imagination, calling successfully for the use of the four-man fighting patrol for reconnaissance into the Indonesian part of Borneo from the spring of 1964. Woodhouse retired from the army in 1965, three months after his last operational patrol.

*BELOW: Time for a quick smoke before carrying out a patrol in the Sarawak region of Borneo in 1963. Sarawak was the focal point of Indonesian incursions – until the SAS put a stop to them.*

*ABOVE: SAS men push a native canoe through rough Borneo water.*

*BELOW: Typical SAS uniform for Borneo – loose and comfortable.*

opposed to the establishment of the Malaysian federation. In early 1963 Indonesian forces started to infiltrate, crossing over the frontier between Kalimantan and the British possessions. Malaysia came into existence in September 1963, with Sabah and Sarawak (although not Brunei and Singapore) within its new borders. Sukarno supplied a Chinese terrorist group based largely in Sarawak, the Clandestine Communist Organisation, with weapons and allowed its members to train in Kalimantan. Empowered to protect the new country's sovereignty, the UK moved to organise a force of British and commonwealth troops to aid the Malaysian forces in north Borneo.

The SAS Regiment's expertise in survival and fighting in a jungle environment were to prove a vital asset Borneo has two distinct types of jungle: primary and secondary. In Borneo's primary jungle, trees attaining a height of 60m (200ft) or more are not unusual, culminating in a dense canopy of leaves through which very little light can penetrates. Visibility can be reduced to 50m (164ft) or less, but the one advantage of this perpetual gloom is that there is little undergrowth to hinder movement. In secondary jungle, a measure of sunlight reaches ground level particularly in areas such as

the banks of a river and where primary jungle has been cleared. The ground here is thickly covered by grasses, ferns and shrubs. Movement is slow and can be very tiring, as it is often necessary to spend hours spent clearing a path with machetes.

The jungles of Borneo are both hot and humid. Troops carrying heavy loads in these conditions sweat

*ABOVE: An SAS soldier in a native kampong sends a radio message to headquarters. The Regiment's presence along the Kalimantan border provided excellent intelligence for regular units.*

*BELOW: 'Hearts and minds' in action. A trooper treats a Dyak tribesman during the Borneo campaign. Patrol medics were instrumental in gaining the trust of the locals.*

profusely. Moreover. disease-carrying bacteria and bit-
ing parasites thrive in a jungle environment ,so soldiers need to be on constant guard against infection.

## ADAPT AND SURVIVE

The nature of the terrain makes it doubly important to
wear the right type of clothing, especially over the
lower half of the body, where strong trousers and
stout boots are vital to protect the legs and feet. There
is a very real risk of walking into the nest of a scorpi-
on or spider – the absence of adequate protection can
be highly uncomfortable, even fatal. The standard
British Army issue boots, with canvas uppers designed
to let the feet breathe, were wholly inadequate, and
most men had cobblers in Singapore make new uppers
of soft leather, or otherwise bought American or
Australian boots with sturdier uppers.

The head also required protection, and the men of
the SAS Regiment soon found that they had to adapt
the issue item to their own requirements by cutting
down the standard British Army 'bush' hat The brim
was so big that it  blocked out what little light the
jungle offered, and often caught on branches.

Legs and arms needed protection from bites and
scratches, so shirt sleeves were always rolled down to
stop insects clinging to the skin and also to prevent
arms coming into contact with some types of foliage,
which could possibly result in a nasty skin rash.

*ABOVE: Patrolling through the Borneo jungle, this SAS troopers
face shows the intense concentration needed to survive in a
what was a highly hostile and threatening environment.*

The task faced by the British and their allies in
Borneo was singularly difficult. Under the command
of Major-General Walter Walker, a mere five battal-
ions of infantry covered some 1500km (930 miles) of
frontier, which was in general unsurveyed in all but
the sketchiest terms and almost wholly covered with
jungle. Along this frontier Walker's forces had to contend with Indonesian forces attempting to infiltrate
into Borneo, and behind the frontier a they had to
deal with a further threat, in the shape of the
Clandestine Communist Organisation (CCO).

In 1963 'A' Squadron of the SAS arrived in Borneo,
under the direction of the Regiment's commanding
officer, Colonel Woodhouse. Major General Walker
initially wanted to employ the SAS as a mobile
reserve, which could be para-dropped onto the jungle
canopy to recapture areas taken by the Indonesians.
Woodhouse was sure that this concept would cause a
high level of casualties, however, and managed to con-
vince Walker that the SAS would be altogether better
suited to small patrols along the border, where they
could secure intelligence about Indonesian incursions.
Although it had only 70 men, by operating in two- or
three-man patrols the squadron was able to deploy 21

patrols along the entire length of the border. They were highly effective as they were able to remain in the jungle for long periods (one patrol stayed in the Long Jawi area of Sarawak for six months) and became familiar with their area and its regular routine.

## 'HEARTS AND MINDS'

Contact with the local inhabitants formed an important part of SAS operations, and the same type of 'hearts and minds' programme that had proved successful in Malaya was soon adopted. Each patrol made immediate contact with the local population and gained its trust: the SAS troopers would often live with the locals, sharing their longhouses and helping with the planting and harvesting of crops. Within each patrol, the trooper most important in the 'hearts and minds' efforts was the medic: his efforts in alleviating the illnesses and injuries of the local population reaped huge benefits when it came to gathering intelligence concerning Indonesian strengths and dispositions later in the campaign.

The first SAS deployment was to Brunei, and once it had arrived A Squadron was soon involved in intelligence-gathering work with the aid of the Border Scouts: indigenous irregular forces whose establishment had been authorised by Walker to provide an intelligence-gathering cordon along the border with Kalimantan. Armed and trained by the SAS as paramilitary forces, the Border Scouts were not combat troops as such. When they did engage Indonesian forces the consequences were often disastrous for them, but when used in their intended role, they were invaluable as the 'eyes and ears' of the defences along the long border. Recruited from the local tribes, individual Scouts were often attached to SAS patrols to

aid communications with the local population (they were later trained for cross-border raids).

During the initial stages of the campaign the role of the SAS was simple and straightforward: collecting intelligence. Indonesian incursions into Sarawak began in April 1963, and Indonesian infiltration along the borders of Sabah and Sarawak became steadily more extensive during the winter of 1963-64. Concentrating on likely points of attack, and as a result of their local knowledge of the terrain and indigenous tribes, the troopers of the SAS now began to assist regular infantrymen in stopping infiltrations by escorting them to ambush sites, and the increasing rate and scale of Indonesian incursion also meant that SAS patrols encountered the enemy more frequently. A trooper from D Squadron relates of one such contact: 'In late 1964 our four-man patrol was heading back to base camp after six days in the *ulu* (jungle). The plan was to get back before last light, but the mountainous countryside and the Indos had other ideas. A rope toggle is standard equipment in the jungle. It is about 5m (16ft) long and is used for crossing fast-flowing rivers or streams by hooking the toggles together. This simple system allows the team to hook up to each other and cross dangerous water with some degree of safety. 'Anyway we reached a section of the river that was narrow but deep. We were armed with Armalites (M16 assault rifles). When the Regiment first arrived in Borneo the SLR [Self-Loading Rifle] was standard issue, but within a short space of time the American Armalite was introduced. Though it doesn't have long range, it is light and compact, and is ideally suited to jungle warfare. We

*Corporal 22 SAS, Borneo, 1965-66. He wears a 1958-pattern webbing belt, fitted to which are ammunition pouches and water bottle. His weapon in the American 5.56mm M16 assault rifle.*

scanned the opposite bank for any signs of an enemy presence. So far, so good. Then, as I prepared to cross over, I saw a black flash on the other side. Before I could react the river bank was being riddled with machine-gun fire, quickly followed by frenzied bursts from the Armalites. Our Iban [native inhabitant of Sarawak] scout had earlier warned us that something was wrong. They were amazing those little guys, they could see and hear things that we would never perceive. I was bloody glad we had them, I can tell you. Anyway, our scout had dived behind this boulder as the GPMG and Armalites put a hail of shot into the space where we had seen the hostile. The Indo didn't have a chance, he went down in an instant.

'The contact was over in seconds and the jungle fell silent. We had killed one Indonesian but there might be more nearby. By this time I had taken cover and, like everyone else, scanned the area for signs of any more of the opposition. Then we quickly bugged out and moved downstream, taking up defensive positions and waiting for the Indos to mount a follow-up ambush. However, they didn't bother and we speedily crossed the river. There is one interesting postscript to the story. Our tracker, who spoke English, said he would check the body. Before we knew what he was up to, he came running back with a big smile on his face. He had cut off the Indo's head and stuffed it into his bag! "Good money, good money," he kept repeating, referring to the bounty he would receive from the Brunei government.'

## CROSS-BORDER RAIDS

At the beginning of the Borneo campaign the SAS Regiment had only two squadrons, but this changed as soon as it became clear that it was achieving excellent results. B Squadron was reformed in January 1964, and in 1966 G Squadron was formed as a new squadron from men of the Guards Independent Parachute Company, which had been undertaking the same type of operation as the SAS.

Because of the substantial rise in enemy activity, it was clear by the winter of 1963-64 that the British would have to go on to the offensive in order to contain the situation. The government therefore authorised Walker in June 1964 to launch clandestine 'Claret' raids across the border to pre-empt the build-up of Indonesian forces in Kalimantan by striking at their forward bases. The first of these attacks was undertaken in June against an Indonesian camp at Nantakor, and was entirely successful. The SAS troopers, who called themselves 'Tip Toe Boys' because of their ability to strike at their target and then disappear, were in general lightly armed and carried minimum in the way of supplies. The SAS Regiment also trained 40 special Border Scouts, henceforward known as Cross-Border Scouts, to support its raids.

A and B Squadrons conducted several cross-border raids in the second half of 1964. B Squadron was concentrated in the Pueh hill range in western Sarawak, which was a route favoured by CCO agents on their way to Lundu on the coast. A Squadron, commanded by Major Peter de la Billière, was replaced by D Squadron during the first part of 1965. Throughout 1965, the SAS units in Borneo continued their efforts to prevent the infiltration of Indonesian forces into Sarawak and Sabah.

The SAS raids continued into 1966, by which time it had become apparent to the Indonesians that the UK's determination to support Malaysia was not wavering and that the war would not be over quickly. The Indonesian military overthrew President Sukarno in March 1966, and hostilities ceased five months later. Once again the SAS had proved its worth.

*RIGHT: SAS soldier with Iban tracker in Borneo. The Regiment's 'hearts and minds' campaign harnessed the skills of the local inhabitants to track and gather intelligence on the Indonesians.*

# CHAPTER 4

# OMAN

## The SAS also fought in the desert during the 1960s and 1970s, again demonstrating its capabilities as a decisive element in defeating insurgents in the small-scale but savage Omani campaigns.

One of the most important capabilities of the SAS, and it is a fact of which the Regiment is rightly proud, is its ability to operate usefully in any terrain at a moment's notice. In 1958, for example, the SAS Regiment was for the most part a collection of 'jungle warriors' from the Malayan 'Emergency', but they quickly adapted to combat in the heat and dryness of the desert of the Sultanate of Oman, on the southeastern corner of the Arabian peninsula. Here, in 1958, the Regiment was called in to support the forces of the Sultan of Oman in a small but

*ABOVE: Captain Peter de la Billière (left) is appraised of the situation by Major Johnny Watts of 22 SAS on the Jebel Akhdar, northern Oman, in December 1958.*

*LEFT: In the late 1950s and early 1970s, the SAS proved itself to be a crack desert warfare unit, able to take on and defeat numerically superior opponents in defence of the Sultan of Oman.*

bitter counter-insurgency campaign fought in the mountainous Jebel Akhdar (Green Mountain) region to the west of the capital, Muscat.

The autocratic rule of the Sultan was being challenged by rebels led by Sulaiman bin Himyar, Ghalib bin Ali and Ghalib's brother, Talib. Insurgents, well armed by local standards, had occupied Jebel Akhdar in the north of the country in 1957 and declared the region independent. The Sultan called for British support and the British Government despatched a brigade of conventional infantry, which quelled the insurrection around Jebel Akhdar. Some insurgents were left ensconced in Jebel Akhdar, an area of some 350 square kilometres (135 square miles) with mountains around a high plateau that could be reached only by small and very easily defended passes. Sooner or later, therefore, the insurrection would have to be ended by an assault on the rebels' central position, a task that seemed fraught with difficulty.

It was inevitable that the SAS, under Lieutenant-Colonel Tony Deane-Drummond, should be chosen as the leading strike element. As a result, 70 troopers of Major John Watts' D Company arrived in Oman during November 1958 and began operations straight away, establishing positions on the northern side of the jebel. In addition to the inhospitable terrain, the SAS troopers had to contend with the good marksmanship of the rebels, and this, together with the lack of cover, made any daylight movement difficult.

In January 1959 the newly arrived A Squadron under Major John Cooper was allocated responsibility for the assault from the north, while D Squadron attacked from the south.

### ASSAULT ON THE JEBEL AKHDAR

The attack went in at 0300 hours on 26 January. It was a difficult climb from the village of Kamah up between the Wadi Kamah and the Wadi Suwaiq, Having spread rumours among the unit's Arab donkey handlers, the SAS ensured that the rebels were expecting an attack from Tanuf in the west, and were deployed accordingly. Three troops of A Squadron fell on Aqabat al Dhafar, while the fourth and last troops, reinforced by the machine guns of the other three

*BELOW: 'Sabrina', one of the SAS objectives during the Jebel Akhdar campaign. This photograph conveys the type of terrain encountered by the Regiment in northern Oman, which its members mastered in a spectacular fashion.*

troops, laid down a barrage on 'Sabrina', as the top of the mountain was nicknamed. The troop under the command of Lieutenant Tony Jeapes reach the top of the pinnacle on the high side of the objective and there killed three or four of the rebels, and then poured such a withering fire down on the main position that the rebels promptly decamped – by morning A Squadron was in full control of 'Sabrina'. This threat from the north persuaded the rebels to weaken their defences elsewhere by detaching men to try to stem any further advance by A Squadron, which had meanwhile left 'Sabrina' for Tanuf, where it arrived by 1800 hours, to link up with D Squadron for the final assault on the rebel positions.

The troopers of both squadrons then embarked in trucks for movement to the assembly area at Kamah. As one troop started a diversionary attack up the Wadi Tanuf, the two squadrons at Tamah, heavily laden with weapons, ammunition and other equipment, started their climb. The earlier ruse had been very effective,and ensured that the troopers met little in the way of opposition. Following the SAS were more British troops and contingents of the Sultan of Oman's Armed Forces.

The resistance of the rebels, who had been taken completely by surprise, soon faded. The troopers of the SAS reached the plateau and started to tackle the last pockets of defiance; as the rebel leaders fled to Saudi Arabia their men were disarmed. The losses of the SAS were a mere two men killed. The Regiment's mission did not end with the assault on the jebel, for the troopers immediately started on a 'hearts and minds' campaign to turn the local inhabitants into supporters of the Sultan.

## THE DHOFAR REVOLT

The SAS returned to Oman in the late 1960s to train Omani forces, and then in larger numbers the following year for a more active role in aiding the suppression of an uprising in the south of the country. This new campaign's key action, which took place at Mirbat on the southern coast of Oman, remains a classic example of the weapons skills and overall calibre of SAS troopers. In addition, it came at a crucial time in the war between the forces of the Sultan of Muscat and Oman and of their communist opposition, the People's Front for the Liberation of the Occupied Arabian Gulf (PFLOAG), and there seems every reason to see the victory at Mirbat in July 1972 as the turning point in a war that was ultimately successful for the Sultan.

The UK had signed a treaty of friendship with the Sultan of Muscat in 1789 to give the Honourable East India Company commercial rights in exchange for the protection of the Royal Navy in Arabian waters. By the twentieth century the pirates had disappeared, but the British were happy to maintain diplomatic ties. With the discovery of oil, Oman acquired huge strategic importance, as the country controls the Straits of Hormuz at the entrance to the Persian Gulf.

A revolt against the repressive policies of the Sultan began in 1962 in Dhofar, a province located in the southwest of the country, bordering Saudi Arabia to the north and the Republic of Yemen to the west. The Dhofar Liberation Front (DLF), demanded the modernisation of the province and the somewhat less definable wish of 'Dhofarisation' or 'Dhofar for the Dhofaris'. Notable for their traditional and strongly Islamic leanings, the men of the DLF were poorly equipped and trained in the conventional military sense. In response to the rising, the Sultan posted about 1000 men of the Sultan of Oman's Armed Forces (SAF) in the area to crush the rebellion. The Omani forces were initially successful, but farther to the west in the Marxist People's Democratic Republic of Yemen (PDRY) further trouble was brewing.

Here another insurrectionist force, the PFLOAG committed itself to the war in Dhofar. The DLF soon found itself absorbed into the larger, more dynamic but fundamentally different PFLOAG, and soon the tide of campaign turned against

*Typical SAS dress on the Jebel Akhdar. This trooper's woollen hat and 'Denison' smock are necessary items to combat the freezing nights. His weapon is the L4A4 machine gun, essentially a modified Bren gun.*

*ABOVE: The village of Saiq, the main rebel base on the Jebel Akhdar. This photograph shows it after being taken by the SAS, and indicates its wretched state following bombing.*

the SAF, which really did not possess either the strength or training to undertake an effective counter-insurgency campaign. By 1970, the PFLOAG, with help from both the USSR and China, had control of the whole of Dhofar. The Sultan was on the verge of total defeat, but then events took a somewhat different turn.

In July 1970, the Sultan was deposed in a bloodless palace coup by his son, Qaboos, who immediately announced a general amnesty and a plan for the major civil development of Oman, with particular emphasis on Dhofar. Within a few hours of the old Sultan's overthrow, the first elements of an increased SAS presence reached Dhofar to bolster the position of the new Sultan and provide support for the SAF, which was already enjoying the benefits of British training after the arrival of a small party from the SAS, now under the command of Lieutenant-Colonel John Watts, in December 1969. These SAS elements were formally designated as British Army Training Teams (BATTs) so the British Government was able to claim there were no British combat troops in Oman.

The SAS set about implementing a 'hearts and minds' policy to run in parallel with the new Sultan's measures to bring his country further into the twentieth century, and the situation in Dhofar seemed to enter a period of increased stability, with the rebels continuing to hold the areas which they had already gained but achieving no further successes. But victory was another matter. The SAS received an unexpected boost in its efforts when a number of *adoo* (the nickname for the rebel soldiers), alienated by the PFLOAG's anti-Islamic Marxist ideology, took advantage of the amnesty to surrender to the government. The leader of the men, Salim Mubarak, advocated

*LEFT: Say cheese! 16 Troop, D Squadron, 22 SAS, in late January 1959, just before their final assault against the rebels. The actual attack involved a nine-hour climb up a goat track.*

turning his men into an anti-rebel group, called a *firqat* (company). The SAS began training Salim's men, and very soon the first of many *firqats*, the Firqat Salahadin, was formed.

## FIVE WAYS TO WIN HEARTS AND MINDS

Watts decided that the key to the situation in Dhofar was to win over the Dhofari population. He devised his 'Five Fronts' plan, whose five elements were an intelligence cell for an accurate determination of the rebel strength and plans, an information team to work on the local population, a medical team to improve life for the local population, a veterinary team to improve the local population's livestock, and wherever possible the enlistment of Dhofaris to fight for the sultan. These five elements were the foundations of the 'hearts and minds' effort that was to play so crucial a part in Dhofari events over the next five years.

The first success gained by a *firqat* was the recapture of Sudh, some 30km (19 miles) east of Mirbat, during February 1971; soon after this, Watts decided that the time was ripe for a switch to offensive operations on the Jebel Dhofar itself, which was the core of the PFLOAG's strength. In March, the SAS and *firqat* launched a probing attack that overcame strong PFLOAG opposition to take the 'Eagle's Nest', a complex of caves and ridges on the edge of the main plateau. The object of this forward move was not merely to drive the PFLOAG back, but to bring the 'Five Fronts' campaign to the Jebel Dhofar; to shield the civil element of this objective, the military line was pushed farther forward in Operation 'Jaguar' in October 1971, when 100 SAS troopers, 250 men of the SAF and 300 men of five *firqats* advanced to take Jibjat and 'White City' and allow the establishment of the 'Leopard Line' of barbed wire, mines and ground sensors designed to prevent the delivery of supplies to the PFLOAG from the PDRY.

By the end of 1971, therefore, the Omani Government had made important advances, moral as well as territorial, in Dhofar. A number of *firqat* groups had been raised and were becoming operational within the context of the SAS's 'Five fronts' 'hearts and minds' programme, whose four other elements were also beginning to achieve significant levels of success. Seeing that the pace of their progress was not just slowing but had in fact been halted and in places driven back, the rebels decided that they required an important victory to persuade the Dhofari population that the rebel cause would eventually triumph. The

rebels accordingly decided to mount an attack against Mirbat, some 65km (40 miles) to the east of Salalah.

## MUCH ADOO IN DHOFAR

The account of the battle that followed is based on first-hand accounts by SAS troopers who fought in Oman. In July 1972, the SAS soldiers had been at Mirbat as the resident BAT Team for three months, training the *firqats* in the use of infantry weapons. The enemy, the *adoo*, were always in the surrounding hills, but the SAS didn't bother about them too much. They would launch the odd artillery attack on Mirbat which usually fell well short, but apart from that it was pretty quiet.

The fact that the SAS troopers had no reconnaissance of the hills around the town could have been disastrous, for it was in these hills that the rebels were putting together a significant quantity of firepower and the men to ensure total victory in the forthcoming battle. The rebels had some 250 men, all seasoned fighters who believed vehemently in their cause. Among their assortment of weapons were Kalashnikov AK-47 automatic rifles, Russian machine guns 75mm recoilless rifles, mortars and Carl Gustav rocket launchers.

*This SAS officer in Aden in the 1960s is wearing loose-fitting jungle trousers and a khaki shirt. His weapon is the 7.62mm Self-Loading Weapon, which has excellent stopping power and good range for desert fighting. On his feet he wears rugged desert boots; his headgear is a jungle hat.*

*ABOVE: Members of the Sultan's Armed Forces (SAF) in Oman in 1971. In general, the SAF worked well with the SAS during the war in southern Oman.*

The SAS soldiers had no idea of what was about to hit them. After an uneventful tour of duty, they were due to leave on 19 July – the same day the *adoo* intended to take the town. 'Far from being a bunch of ill-armed bandits, the *adoo* carefully planned their attack on Mirbat. They knew the bad weather would prevent any air cover from the Omani Air Force based at nearby Salalah, and it would also stop any SAS reinforcements being flown in by helicopter. Like all guerrilla groups, the *adoo* had a good intelligence network and they knew when SAS teams were being rotated. The Omanis are notorious gossips, and although the SAS men used the grapevine for their own purposes, there was nothing they could do to stop the reverse happening.'

The SAS team at Mirbat was not completely on its own, however, for other elements of the defence force included 30 askars (tribesmen) and 25 paramilitary police, equipped with elderly Lee-Enfield bolt-action rifles, holding the Wali's Fort and the Dhofar Gendarmerie (DG) Fort respectively. A few *adoo* had allowed themselves to be seen by the defence, however, which had sent a group of 60 *firqat*s to check them out, and this weakened the garrison.

The defence was not wholly lacking in heavier weapons, however, for there was an elderly 25-pounder field gun in a sandbagged pit beside the DG

Fort, and an 81mm mortar in a sandbagged pit beside the Batthouse, as the BATT's headquarters was known. On the roof of the Batthouse itself was a 7.62mm GPMG and a 0.5in Browning heavy machine gun.

'Just before dawn on 19 July the *adoo* began their attack. It was just before 0530 hours, the time when they could make the maximum use of the uncertain light, which, combined with the poor weather, meant it was almost impossible for the sentries to spot their stealthy advance.

'Some 1000m north of the perimeter wire, which protected the team's area, the *adoo* cut down eight Dhofar gendarmes who were patrolling on the Jebel Ali. Kealy rushed to the roof of the Batthouse to see what was happening.'

The SAS soldiers scanned the scene. The Wali's Fort was near the shoreline of Mirbat Bay and contained the askars. To the northeast lay the Gendarmerie Fort, which held around 25 men, though they were only armed with Lee-Enfields. Suddenly the *adoo* appeared, ghost-like, out of the early morning haze: lines of men armed with automatic rifles advancing steadily towards Mirbat. Moments later there was a deafening roar of gun and mortar fire as the *adoo* opened up. The battle had begun.

*This SAS soldier in Oman in the early 1970s is equipped with a water bottle, ammunition pouches and an escape-and-evasion kit fixed to his belt. His heavy bergen contains extra clothing, rations and ammunition for his M16 rifle.*

*ABOVE: The Omani Government stronghold at Taqa, Dhofar province (note the sandbagged tower). The SAS barracks is situated in the buildings in the bottom left of the photograph.*

The odds were not very good. On the roof were Captain Kealy, Corporal Pete Wignall, Trooper Tobin, Trooper Savesaki and Corporal Roger Chapman. They had two machine guns on the roof – a GPMG and a Browning gun – and they were to play a crucial part in the battle. Beside the Batthouse, in a sandbagged pit, Lance-Corporal Harris manned the 81mm mortar. As soon as the fighting had started, Corporal Labalaba, a huge Fijian, had sprinted over to man the 25-pounder beside the Dhofar Gendarmerie Fort alongside the Omani gunner.

## MIRBAT UNDER FIRE

The controlled fire from the Batthouse began to take affect: *adoo* fighters started to go down as they were hit by double taps and short machine-gun bursts, but still the enemy kept coming. All the SAS positions were under heavy fire now, and the forts were taking hits from rockets and mortar bombs. The lone SAS mortar was replying, and in the distance the 25-pounder was frantically firing into the enemy ranks.

The situation of the SAS and its Omani allies was bad, for the *adoo* were using all their considerable fire-power. Kealy must have appreciated that this was in

no way a probing attack, for the number of *adoo* was altogether too great for that. He radioed the provincial headquarters in Salalah with the news of what was happening, which was now that the Wali's Fort, DG Fort, Batthouse and even Mirbat town were now all under attack. The SAS was in effect surrounded on three sides, but with its local allies was holding on. But how long could the *adoo* be held at bay?

'Kealy requested an air strike, but he knew that it was a forlorn hope because of the weather – the *adoo* had played their trump card and it was working. Rockets slammed into the DG Fort, sending masonry into the air and leaving gaping holes in its wall. Then its tower disappeared in a pall of smoke and dust. By this time the walls were riddled with hundreds of bullets. How much more could it take?

'Over the radio came the message that Laba had been hit. The 25-pounder had gone quiet. Laba had been hit in the chin, but with remarkable composure all he would say was "enemy are getting a bit close".

## JOHNNY COOPER

An original member of L Detachment in World War II, Johnny Cooper joined the unit from the Scots Guards and No 8 (Guards) Commando At the beginning of 1951, Cooper rejoined the regular army and was posted to Malaya to serve with 22 SAS Regiment. In January 1959, Cooper was suddenly sent to Oman, where he was involved in one of the SAS Regiment's most celebrated operations, the storming of the Jebel Akhdar. In 1960 Cooper left 22 SAS to take up the post of company commander of the Omani Northern Frontier Regiment, and then second-in-command of the Muscat Regiment. This multi-talented officer soon returned to the SAS , however, and in 1963 led a covert mission into Yemen after a left wing coup, to discover the precise nature of Egyptian involvement, and to help forces loyal to the government. Cooper had three spells in the Yemen before completing his mission in the early part of 1966.

Batthouse requesting an immediate air strike. At that moment Labalaba was again shot and this time killed, and the *adoo* began to close in on the gunpit. Tobin was shot, and both the gunpit and DG Fort were being pounded by rockets as well as gunfire. Firing with commendable coolness, Savesaki and Kealy picked off individual *adoo*, but then a grenade was lobbed into the pit. The grenade miraculously failed to detonate, but now Kealy and his surviving men needed another miracle to save them. They got it.'

From nowhere, two Omani Strikemaster jets appeared, streaking their way overhead and heading for the enemy. They poured cannon fire into the *adoo*, and halted he enemy attack. Kealy radioed for Harris to hit targets near him, but they were so close that he had to haul the barrel up to his chest and grip the weapon with his legs before he could fire it.

At Salalah the 24 members of G Squadron had embarked as rapidly as possible into helicopters, which were flying to Mirbat as another attack by the Strikemaster light attack aircraft inflicted further casualties on the *adoo*. G Squadron arrived, troopers, who were fresh and heavily armed. They cleared *adoo* from around the Dhofar Gendarmerie Fort.

The SAS had lost two men dead – Corporal Labalaba and Trooper Tobin – and two more men seri-

Savesaki volunteered to get some medical aid to his compatriot. Kealy agreed. Savesaki raced off towards the gunpit. Bullets whistled around him as he dodged and weaved his way forward.

'In the gunpit Savesaki had used a dressing to staunch the flow of blood from Labalaba's face. The Omani gunner had also been shot and seriously wounded, and the 25-pounder's shield had been riddled with bullets. Then Savesaki was shot in the shoulder and head, and fell back against the sandbags that protected the position. He was still able to fire his weapon, though, and Labalaba continued to load the gun on his own.

'Unable to contact the gunpit or the DG Fort, Kealy decided to go to the fort, taking with him only one other man, Trooper Tobin. The helicopter then appeared out of the cloud, but as it tried to swoop in to land it was driven back by fire from the massed *adoo*. This seemed to spur the *adoo* into a fresh effort, thinking that victory would come from a last push.

'Kealy and Tobin reached the gunpit and took over from the two wounded Fijians. From the 25-pounder's ammunition bunker Kealy sent a radio message to the

*ABOVE: The portrait of Corporal Labalaba commissioned by the Fijian Government after his heroic actions at the Battle of Mirbat on 19 July 1972, in which he lost his life.*

*ABOVE: The Dhofar Gendarmerie (DG) Fort at Mirbat. It was the focal point of the adoo attacks during the battle, as it dominated the Mirbat itself and the other defensive positions.*

*BELOW: The remains of the gunpit beside the DG Fort at Mirbat. The 25-pound field gun manned by Labalaba was situated here; during the battle it was subject to ferocious attacks.*

ously wounded, but the cost to the enemy had been far greater: over 30 dead were discovered on the battlefield alone.

Far more important to the rebels, however, was the loss of prestige that they suffered as a result of their failure at Mirbat. Not only had they lost many of their best men, but insult was added to injury by the fact that they had outnumbered their enemies to a very marked degree. Far from convincing the Dhofaris that the Sultan and his British supporters were finished, the battle at Mirbat effectively destroyed the credibility of the PFLOAG.

In the aftermath of the battle the civil aid programme was increased in scope to ensure that the quality of life of the average Dhofari was appreciably improved, and as a result there were more *adoo* defections as the men of the SAS and their Omani allies continued to take the war to the enemy. In 1973 the SAS and an Iranian battalion loaned by the Iranian Government to man the 'Hornbeam Line' cooperated in the clearance of the region between Salalah and the Thamrait road. In the following year, an offensive by seven SAS teams and several *firqats* in the northeastern part of the Jebel Dhofar eliminated the rebels from the valleys of central Dhofar. By 1975 the surviving strength of the PFLOAG was being driven back towards the border with the PDRY. In October of that year, the PDRY withdrew elements of its regular army, recognising that it had effectively lost the war. The SAS squadrons were pulled out of Oman in September 1976, having quelled the revolt and won the war.

# CHAPTER 5

# NORTHERN IRELAND

## In the troubles of Northern Ireland the SAS played an important part gathering vital intelligence; it also became notorious, even controversial, after bloody ambushes of IRA terrorist groups.

The SAS has fought its longest campaign in Northern Ireland. Although life is quieter in the late 1990s than at any time in the past quarter century, there remains the possibility that the current uneasy peace is no more than a lull in the agonised history of Ulster. It is impossible in the space available to provide more than a sketch of the Regiment's activities in the province, but it is possible to convey an impression of the type of war waged by the Regiment in Ulster and the kind of skills needed to fight the 'unseen enemy' there.

*ABOVE: A patrol waits to be extracted following a mission in Northern Ireland. The SAS makes great use of helicopter transport in Ulster, especially from the large British Army heliport at Bessbrook.*

*LEFT: The SAS fights two types of war in Northern Ireland against Nationalist terrorists: in the towns and cities, and in the country-side. It is a deadly, and never-ending, cat-and-mouse game.*

British troops were first despatched to Northern Ireland in August 1969 in an effort to check the increasing violence between the Catholic and Protestant communities. This period also saw the first deployment of the SAS, when members of D Squadron were used in the hunt for Protestant weapons thought to be hidden in the country-side. At this time there were considerable demands on the Regiment due to the war in Oman. This meant the Regiment could not maintain a sizeable presence in Northern Ireland, although individual officers and non-commissioned officers were posted to the province for the implementation of specific reconnaissance tasks. In 1976, however, the British Government announced that the SAS was indeed deployed in Northern Ireland, and this indicated the start of a squadron-sized SAS presence in Ulster.

The SAS's main opponents in Northern Ireland were the nationalist terrorists of the Irish Republican Army

*ABOVE: A British Army vehicle checkpoint in South Armagh. This is an area of high Irish Republican Army (IRA) activity. As a result, it was the location of the SAS's first major deployment.*

(IRA), who were trying to drive the British out of Northern Ireland by force, and the smaller Irish National Liberation Army (INLA), an organisation with Marxist leanings. (There was little SAS activity against Protestant terrorist organisations because these groups were not fighting the security forces.)

### WATCHING THE TERRORISTS

South Armagh was a hotbed of IRA activity during the mid-1970s, but the use of the SAS in this area resulted in a temporary reduction in terrorist activity. In one incident, Peter Cleary, a senior IRA 'player', was captured near Forkhill, but was then killed as he tried to escape. Despite the success of the SAS in this single incident, however, the terrorist threat was not a problem that was ever likely to disappear without a struggle, and the SAS accordingly prepared itself for a protracted effort against the terrorists. The primary tasks of the SAS in Northern Ireland were, and are, surveillance and intelligence gathering, although the men of the Regiment also perform ambush operations when called upon to do so.

From the late 1970s, the SAS deployment in Ulster was one troop (usually 16 men) at Bessbrook under the command of the 3rd Infantry Brigade, one troop in the Belfast area under the command of the 39th

Infantry Brigade, one troop in Londonderry under the command of the 8th Infantry Brigade, and one troop under the control of the Commander of Land Forces in Northern Ireland for any operations that this officer might specify. In the 1980s, there was a change in the deployment pattern, however, as the separation of the relevant squadron's troops into different areas had resulted in a dilution of the SAS's capabilities. Recognising this factor, the army asked for the creation of one SAS unit of smaller size, but which could be redeployed from one location to another at short notice as and when required.

The SAS Regiment itself was also running into problems: the Northern Ireland tour for each squadron lasted between four and six months, with periods of acclimatisation training and leave before and after it respectively. With only four operational squadrons, the Regiment found it had a significant part of its strength in Northern Ireland, and this was not a good idea for a unit that has necessarily to keep its men at a high level of proficiency in a large and varied assortment of military skills. The solution to the needs of the army and the SAS was found in the establishment of a new organisation, the Intelligence and Security Group (Northern Ireland) that was generally known as 'The Group'. The result of this change was a reduction in the number of SAS troopers serving in Northern Ireland, from a full squadron to a troop of just over 20 men in Ulster Troop.

By the mid-1980s, SAS troopers were serving for a period of one year in Ulster Troop, and were also collaborating closely within the Group with the 14th Intelligence Unit, a covert army intelligence-gathering organisation created in the early 1970s, whose recruits are trained by the SAS. Within the Group the SAS contingent and 14th Intelligence Unit were commanded by a single officer, and the activities of the Group were highly integrated with those of the special units of the Royal Ulster Constabulary (RUC).

The key to success for the security forces in Northern Ireland is intelligence. In theory, there is complete cooperation and collaboration between all the military and intelligence agencies in Ulster, but there were and are deep suspicions that many of the different agencies were in fact competing with each

## OPERATIONAL BACKGROUND

The 'Troubles' in Northern Ireland began in 1968, with civil rights disturbances prompted by the political and economic aspirations of the Roman Catholic minority. These were manipulated by the Provisional Wing of the Irish Republican Army (IRA), as part of its effort to drive the British out of Northern Ireland so that it could be joined with the Republic or Ireland. British troops were deployed to the Province for security purposes for the first time in 1969, and from then until 1995 the 'Troubles' developed into a three-way struggle between the IRA, the loyalist terror groups opposed to the IRA, and the security forces combating both these primary groups and their various splinter organisations. Within this campaign, the SAS was used mainly for intelligence-gathering purposes and the defeat of armed gangs of the IRA.

*BELOW: A British Army observation post in South Armagh, nicknamed 'bandit country' because of its terrorist activity. The SAS has carried out many rural operations in this area.*

other. MI6, the British intelligence-gathering organisation, for example, often prevented the Special Branch of the RUC from accessing certain information, and the RUC in turn often jealously guarded its own intelligence. Both of these organisations initially disapproved of the SAS Regiment's commitment to Northern Ireland on the basis it indicated the authorities thought their efforts were inadequate. Despite a veneer of unity, therefore, there is every evidence that the rivalry and jealousy between the intelligence-gathering agencies continued to the detriment of the primary task in hand.

## COMBATING THE PROVOS

In Northern Ireland the SAS operated with as great a degree of covertness as was humanly possible. During the SAS's first official tour of duty in the province, for example, troopers of D Squadron were attached to 40 Commando of the Royal Marines in South Armagh. On the ferry to Belfast they were wearing the Royal Marines' green berets and standard disruptive-pattern material (DPM) smocks, and several carried L42 sniper rifles. During this tour the SAS carried out a total of 31 operations.

Most of the IRA's major 'players' were and are known to the security forces by name if not actually by appearance, but the difficulty lay in catching them committing a terrorist offence, for this was the only way in which they could be legally arrested.

SAS troopers are trained to survive and fight in all conditions of weather and climate, and therefore have available to them a wide assortment of specialised clothing, although the requirements of the mission are always placed before other considerations in the selection of clothing and other kit. This is the case in Ulster, as a trooper who served there states: 'We didn't wear anything that made a noise. Boots have been a problem since the British Army was formed, and so many blokes in the Regiment buy their own, particularly US Marine jungle boots, which provide plenty of movement for the ankle but still have a strong base. But we all wore "goon boots", which were small, pullover shoe covers that had lumps of rubber on the sole. The aim was not to leave footprints as the local farmers, Fenian to a man, were quick to spot boot marks and would pass the information on to their mates in the IRA.

'Everything was camouflaged: bergens, weapons, the lot. We added a few extras to our smocks, such as a large inside pocket to carry a small radio and a few

## RICHARD WESTMACOTT

One of the first SAS casualties in Northern Ireland, Captain Richard Westmacott was leading an eight-man SAS unit operating in two unmarked cars in Belfast on 2 May 1980. The soldiers were in plain clothes, but were armed with handguns and automatic weapons. Receiving instructions by radio to go to a house in Antrim Road, Westmacott was in the first car that drew to a halt in front of the house shortly after 2pm. Four armed IRA terrorists who had escaped from custody, were inside, and opened fire as soon as the men got out the car. Westmacott was killed instantly. The SAS men thought that the fire was coming from No 369, which they stormed. The terrorists were actually next door in No 371. Army and Royal Ulster Constabulary units sealed off the area as soon as the shooting started, and the gunmen surrendered. This incident shows that in the early 1980s the SAS was still refining the tactics for successful operation in Northern Ireland. Later it would be inconceivable for a unit to intervene instantly, rather than placing the house under surveillance pending later action.

batteries. In the main, though, we wore the same uniform as other British Army units. This was because if a team decided to break cover, they would look like ordinary squaddies.'

Observation Post (OP) work is the SAS's main task in Northern Ireland, as SAS troopers have the combination of training with mental and physical endurance to survive in confined and highly uncomfortable OPs for days on end. Many OP missions are conducted from Bessbrook, the headquarters for SAS operations in South Armagh: an SAS trooper describes a typical OP mission mounted from the 'Mill':

'After an intelligence brief at the Mill we flew by Wessex to Crossmaglen SF (security forces) base, where we were due to meet one of our teams that had just spent several days on the ground. Once inside the base, we were briefed by the company commander of the Black Watch and an RUC officer. The aim of this was to update us on their activity in the area and the day's events at local level. Our people passed on details about known "players" seen in the TAOR (Tactical Area Of Responsibility), and the movements of "targets" the Provos had been monitoring.

'The deployment of the OP had been sanctioned after intelligence from Special Branch indicated a big hit was being planned against Cross. In the past Provo machine-gun attacks had scored massive publicity, but their favoured method was to use mortars. They weren't very accurate, but Paddy would lob a few shells in to scare the shit out of everyone and remind the British Army that it was in enemy territory.

## COVERT OPERATIONS

'We had been told by the intelligence boys that the attack would be very big, and the Provos had even been boasting in the local pubs that at least 10 British soldiers would die, so the heat was on to prevent it happening. There were only two places from where the Provos could launch such an attack, the most likely being a football field behind the base.'

The creation of a covert OP is not easy, for it requires the location of a position from which the SAS team can keep watch over the target right round the clock, but allowing secret access for the members of the team. In South Armagh and places like it, where virtually every member of the civil population is hostile, this raised even more acute difficulties and required the use of elaborate deceptive measures.

'A disused house on the edge of Crossmaglen provided the perfect position for a long-term OP. It was detached and isolated on one side of the road, with an occupied dwelling just 100m (328ft) away. The obvious dangers of inserting a team into such a position required a check by an EOD [explosive ordnance disposal] team. We left Cross late in the afternoon as part of a Black Watch patrol, also taking three Royal Engineers along with us.'

Total vigilance is a necessary feature of covert operations in Ulster as the terrorists have informants everywhere. Moreover, the standard operating procedures (SOPs) applicable to Belfast and other built-up areas are not always desirable in rural regions and villages. It was not easy to operate Q cars and other such covert vehicles in Crossmaglen, for instance, as the place is so small and the security forces' base is watched the

ABOVE: *The SAS's enemy in Northern Ireland – an IRA terrorist. The IRA's operatives are well trained, motivated and equipped, and have proved to be the Regiment's most persistent foes.*

whole time by Republican 'spotters'. The SAS therefore frequently uses helicopters and foot patrols as a means of introducing teams into OPs without attracting attention.

'We carried everything we would need to sustain a 10-day observation: water, food, ammunition and surveillance equipment, as well as a variety of "live traps" which we planted around the building as "insurance" against any nosy Provos who paid us an unannounced visit. We also had an escape route in case we were compromised.

'Living in a covert OP for 10 days in conditions where you could be compromised at any time by noise or smell is very stressful, especially if your "hide" is near an inhabited building. Noise is a killer, and so a variety of precautions are taken to avoid compromise, and these must be enforced at all times if success is going to be achieved.

*ABOVE: SAS patrols operate covertly in Nationalist areas of Northern Ireland, either from observation posts in buildings or in plainclothes in unmarked civilian cars and vans.*

'After entering the building the bergens are placed in ready-to-move positions and are never moved again. Soft shoes, trainers or desert boots are put on and combat boots are stowed away – they are too heavy and difficult to sleep in. We had one collapsible camp bed, which we had "liberated" from an American para, and erected it straight away. Cameras and night scopes were set up and plastic bags for human waste were put to one side. A second bag for empty food cans was also put to one side. It is imperative to trap all smells – like noise they can literally be a killer. They can attract dogs and cats which will compromise the operation.'

In any OP there is little to do except make the considerable effort to keep alert, and this is important as lapses of concentration can be lethal. Another factor that had always to be expected and therefore prevented is the tendency of men to take risks merely as a means of alleviating the boredom of life in an OP. The avoidance of these and similar dangers places great emphasis on the individual trooper's self-determination. Moreover, it is always in the men's minds that they may be discovered.

'Camouflage cream is a must at all times for two reasons. First, although we could not see any broken or damaged tiles, a white face shines and might therefore be seen by a passer-by. Second, if someone accidentally entered the property and compromised our operation we needed the element of shock to surprise them.

'Wearing desert boots, combat trousers, black rollneck jumpers and woolly hats kept us warm, and gave us the opportunity to move about quietly. We weren't too worried about getting bumped by the opposition because we each had a fully loaded 9mm Browning High Power in a shoulder holster and our main weapons were always close by.

## OPERATIONAL PROCEDURE

'To give us an arc of observation for the scope and camera we removed a small part of a brick, which gave us plenty of vision to monitor the road, the houses and the potential mortar baseplate on the playing fields. Nobody talks during the day unless it is vital, and operational details such as DLB [dead letter box – a point used for the dropping off of supplies] arrangements are made by whisper. At night one of our teams at Cross mounted DLBs in which they delivered fresh sandwiches and supplies, such as radio batteries and other items, and took away our waste. This procedure centred on prearranged Rvs [rendezvous], which often gave us the chance to exchange operational details and receive additional orders. Goods were exchanged or left in a bergen, and we in turn would deliver bergens full of waste, as well as 'shot' film that had to be returned for developing as quickly as possible.'

## WEAPONS, COMMUNICATIONS...AND RATS

The troopers of the SAS are combat soldiers as well as intelligence gatherers, so the state of his weapon is always very important to the individual trooper and by extension to his comrades as well.

'Magazines on our weapons were changed every day, because a sustained period in an OP can cause the mag spring to seize and result in a stoppage ... In Ulster most of the blokes like the M16 because it can deliver more rounds than the SLR or even the new SA-80. It's also fairly small, making it useful for OP work in a covert "hide". An increasingly popular weapon with the Regiment in Ulster is the Heckler & Koch 53, which is basically a scaled-down version of the G3 rifle, though it also looks like the MP5.'

The communication of information to headquarters could often be very troublesome because of one-way or mutual interference.

'VHF, for example, often interfered with local television sets when they were switched on and basically told the locals that the military were in the area. Thus if you are operating from a property you never transmit during daylight hours if you can help it.'

OP work is always very hard on the nerves, but despite this factor the men in a covert OP still need to attend to the daily maintenance of their site if the OP was not to be compromised.

'Our rubbish and human waste was bagged up and sealed all the time. Our urine was bottled and food packed in plastic containers, but the rats still found us. Rats are a major problem in OP work around Cross, and their presence can cause you to make noise in an effort to stop them attacking waste and refuse ... They were big and would stop at nothing to get at the food or rubbish we had.

'We asked Cross to supply rat poison in a future DLB, which eventually resulted in a bag of 17 rats being shipped back to base in a bergen. The boys back at Cross thought it was some sort of joke, but in fact it was a real problem because we couldn't just

*RIGHT: Plainclothes operatives always go armed in Ulster. For SAS soldiers, blending in with the locals takes a lot of training and resourcefulness. On the streets, one mistake can be fatal.*

leave them in the OP. By the time the operation finished we had returned more than 90 dead rats.'

The systems for supplying covert OPs were constantly tested and modified as required, and they were wholly vital to survival and success. In the 1970s, the DLB system was used, but the risk of this being a target for an IRA ambush meant the Live Letter Box (LLB) method was then adopted.

'The LLB system is much better. A covert car will drive to a pre-arranged RV with its rear window down (there's always two blokes in the front of the car), with another car, a back-up, some distance behind. Anything that has to be got rid of – exposed film, waste, wet sleeping bags – will be thrown onto the back seat of the car, while the bloke in the front passenger seat will pass the stuff requested by the patrol out of his window to the patrol members. Then they will be off.'

Dangerous and tedious, OP work is vital to the intelligence war against the terrorists, and is certainly the best 'weapon' available to the security forces.

Ambush operations were another important aspect of the war waged by the SAS against terrorism. But while ambushes can be enormously successful in operational terms, they can also be controversial in political terms, and, as discovered by the SAS in Northern Ireland, can lead to claims of a 'shoot to kill' policy. The Regiment was fully conscious of the fact that any ambush would be the subject of legal scrutiny, however, and impressed upon its men the importance of sticking closely to the army's rules of engagement.

### SAS AMBUSH

The problems attendant on ambushes can be seen in the details of an operation mounted in County Tyrone during August 1988. The origins of the episode can be traced to June of the same year, when British intelligence first became aware of an imminent IRA operation to murder a former RUC officer who worked in Omagh. In collaboration with the army, the intelligence agencies and the RUC, the SAS planned to set an ambush to prevent the murder attempt by the Mid-Tyrone Brigade of the IRA, comprising Martin Harte, Gerald Harte and Brian Mullen. The security forces informed the intended victim of the IRA's plan, and this former policeman agreed to continue driving his truck to work along his regular route to establish a

*ABOVE: Observation post (OP) work is boring and dangerous, but vital in the war against the IRA. Only meticulous intelligence-gathering can give the SAS the edge over the terrorists.*

movement pattern which would be observed by the terrorists and used in the creation of their attack plan.

The counter-plan devised by the SAS was for the truck to 'break down' near a pre-positioned team that would remain in position and wait for the IRA hit squad to make its appearance. It then transpired that the Mid-Tyrone Brigade was not planning any such operation in the short term, however, for on 20 August 1988 it blew up a coach carrying 35 members of the 1st Battalion, The Light Infantry, as it moved between Aldergrove Airport and the barracks in Omagh. The IRA team used nearly 100kg (220lb) of Semtex plastic explosive in the attack, which killed eight and seriously injured many more.

The SAS did not let the incident alter its plans: the operation went ahead as planned. The terrorists returned to their arms cache on 29 August, and this suggested that the murder attempt would be made on the following day. During the early hours of 30 August an SAS trooper took the place of the target and drove the truck to the pre-planned ambush point. At the same time, a three-man SAS team, with

Browning High Power handguns and 9mm Heckler & Koch MP5 submachine guns, left the barracks in Omagh and walked to a derelict farmhouse near the village of Drumnakilly. Reaching the site, one member of the SAS team hid in a barn while the other two concealed themselves in the hedgerows.

The truck halted outside the farmhouse at about 1900 hours and the 'driver' got out of the cab and unloaded the spare wheel to give the impression he had suffered a flat tyre. All the SAS troopers involved knew that the IRA would soon know of the man's location as Republican informants lived all over the area. Later in the day the terrorists hijacked a white Ford Sierra car and drove to the position of the 'broken down' truck, armed with Kalashnikov AK-47 assault rifles and Webley revolvers.

### REVENGE KILLING

The security forces had been trailing the IRA team earlier on the day of the ambush so that they could keep the SAS troopers informed of their opposition's location. The surveillance was abandoned when it was suspected that one of the unmarked cars had been

*BELOW: In Ulster, the SAS has frequently attached its men to British Army patrols. In this way, routine searches can be used to insert teams covertly into buildings to set up OPs.*

### GIBRALTAR

On 4 March 1988, an IRA active service unit comprising two men and a woman flew independently into Malaga Airport in southern Spain. Their aim was to detonate a Semtex bomb in nearby Gibraltar. Excellent surveillance work, however, meant that they were under surveillance, even before they left Ireland. In nearby Marbella, the IRA rigged a hired Ford Fiesta with 65kg (140lb) of Semtex, enough to demolish a multi-storey building, then left it in a Spanish car park. Another hired car, a Renault, was driven into Gibraltar and parked to 'reserve' a space for the car bomb. The following day the terrorists returned to the Renault on foot. The British assumed this car contained the bomb. Two four-man SAS sticks were tailing them, and when they headed back for the border, one moved in to arrest them. As the troopers closed in, a police siren 'twitched' the terrorists who spotted their followers. One, McCann, made a rapid arm movement, and the soldier opened fire. In court later the trooper stated that he thought the terrorist was about to trigger the bomb by radio. The others, Farrell and Savage, were also gunned down by the troopers following them. When searched, however, all three were found to be unarmed, and without the bomb trigger.

identified by a potential hostile, however, and from that time onwards the SAS team was effectively blind. At the truck, therefore, the SAS man did not appreciate the nature of the Sierra as it raced towards him, but then sensed that something was wrong: as the IRA men opened up with automatic fire, he made a successful dash for the cover of a nearby wall.

The Sierra screeched to a halt, and as the terrorists prepared to disembark and kill their victim, they were hit by a barrage of 9mm fire from the hidden SAS troopers. All three terrorists were killed instantly, effectively ending the existence of the Mid-Tyrone Brigade of the IRA. The SAS soldiers radioed for a Lynx helicopter to lift them out as RUC and army units sealed off the area.

The operation had been a stunning success at the operational level, but almost immediately became a political and media disaster as the British Government remained silent in the face of media and republican outrage for what they saw as a 'revenge killing' for the bus bombing.

In the period between late 1986 and early 1987, the IRA had stepped up the pace and intensity of its terror campaign in Northern Ireland with a series of brutal bombings, beatings and murders as the republican movement attempted to render Ulster ungovernable. The security forces were therefore at a state of high alert and were delighted when, in the course of a routine surveillance, an IRA member was overheard on the telephone talking about a planned attack by the East Tyrone Brigade on the RUC station at Loughall in Country Armagh.

Within the IRA the East Tyrone Brigade was known as the 'A' Team, as it had succeeded in carrying out several audacious attacks against the RUC and the British Army: in December 1985, for example, it had attacked the RUC barracks at Ballygawley with AK-47 and Armalite assault rifles, first killing the two guards on the gate and then raking the barracks before planting a large bomb inside the building. The subsequent explosion totally destroyed the barracks.

The attack on Loughall would be similar in concept, but the SAS and RUC would be ready and waiting. Loughall is a small Protestant enclave in a mainly Catholic area. The village was therefore seen by the Republican movement as a symbol of Protestant (and

thus English) power, the more so as it had been the birthplace of the Orange Order. It had also been relatively untouched by the 'Troubles' up to this time, but the IRA was now determined to alter that with an attack on the police station, which was manned only on a part-time basis.

The gravity of the situation persuaded the SAS to take no chances, so Ulster Troop was reinforced with additional troopers from England. The 16-man troop from 'D' Squadron arrived before Operation 'Judy', as the planned ambush of the IRA at Loughall was code-named, started. Because of the failure of IRA security, the authorities knew that the attack was planned for 8 May; a force of SAS troopers and RUC snipers was infiltrated into the area many hours before the IRA terrorists were due to make an appearance.

The SAS detachment was led by an experienced Ulster Troop staff sergeant. At the briefing the men

*RIGHT: At Loughall, the SAS deployed two full-strength troops to ambush the IRA's East Tyrone Brigade. The SAS force was heavily armed with machine guns and assault rifles.*

were told that the mission was an OP/React (Observation Post able to React), which is the term for an ambush: the IRA would drive into a pre-arranged killing ground where they would be engaged and destroyed.

The men of the SAS force were heavily armed: those of Ulster Troop were carrying Heckler & Koch G3 rifles and those from England had M16 rifles, and there were at least two General Purpose Machine Guns. The men were deployed in two groups: the larger was deployed in the copse overlooking the RUC station close to the Armagh road so that the SAS men, including the two GPMGs, could concentrate fire on the football field in front of the police station. The smaller group was located in the station itself as far from the gates as possible. There were also at least two cut-off groups in the village and another SAS unit close to the church.

The IRA team approached its target in two vehicles, and the operation resulted in the death of eight terrorists. Unfortunately this was not the end of the killing,

*RIGHT: The view at Loughall after the SAS ambush, looking up from the RUC station to the copse where the SAS positioned its two GPMGs to pour fire down on the IRA team.*

*ABOVE: The Toyota van used by the IRA to transport its men to Loughall. Caught in a hail of SAS gunfire during the ambush, it was riddled with bullets, which killed all those inside.*

however, for a Citroen car carrying two brothers, Oliver and Anthony Hughes, was fired upon by the cut-off groups in the mistaken belief that it contained IRA terrorists, and one of them was killed.

After the shooting, the SAS soldiers were evacuated by helicopter after ensuring that the terrorist threat had disappeared. The SAS Regiment had fought its most successful battle in Northern Ireland.

# CHAPTER 6

# THE FALKLANDS WAR

## In the grim South Atlantic winter of 1982, the SAS was a key element in the British recapture of the Falkland Islands. Vital reconnaissance and important raids by the Regiment ensured British success.

In 1982, the military junta ruling Argentina sought to end its increasing unpopularity at home with a 'foreign adventure': the capture of the Falkland Islands. Lying off the southeast coast of Argentina, these islands have long been claimed as Argentine territory and in April 1982 were seized by an Argentine invasion force.

The Argentine move came as an enormous shock to the British Government, and Prime Minister Margaret Thatcher decided that the islands should be brought back under British rule, by force if necessary. It was the opin-

*ABOVE: HMS* Hermes *battles her way south during the early stages of the Falklands War. She left Portsmouth on 5 April 1982 with a detachment of SAS soldiers on board.*

*LEFT: A patrol at dusk on East Falkland. SAS teams were put on the Falklands from the beginning of May 1982 to collect intelligence concerning Argentine strengths and dispositions.*

ion of most in high places that Argentina would capitulate to a show of British force, and a comparatively small Royal Navy task force was created to sail south with an amphibious capability provided by the Royal Marines with a reinforcement of British Army units.

The Falkland Islands were not an ideal battleground for the British. They are some 13,000km (8080 miles) from the UK, and this represented a truly formidable logistical problem. The Ministry of Defence had to create a task force capable of undertaking an amphibious operation a vast distance from home and without the support of big aircraft carriers capable of operating conventional fixed-wing aircraft. Despite the simmering dispute with Argentina about the Falkland Islands over the previous years, however, the British armed forces had no contingency plans for an Argentine invasion. Military thinking was centred on the confrontations that might take place in Europe between NATO and the Warsaw Pact.

The planners also had to take into account the climate and geography of the islands, which were in the grip of an approaching South Atlantic winter and therefore cold, wet and windy, with terrain that consists mostly of treeless moorland and rocky hills.

## SOUTH GEORGIA ON THEIR MINDS

For special forces such as the SAS, the geography of the area is a nightmare. Nevertheless, as soon as he heard about the Argentinian landings, Lieutenant-Colonel Michael Rose, commanding officer of 22 SAS Regiment, offered his unit's services to Brigadier Julian Thompson, the commander of 3 Commando Brigade, entrusted with the task of taking and holding a British beachhead if required. Rose had full confidence in the capabilities of his men, even in the climate and terrain of the Falklands. The SAS was ideally suited to intelligence-gathering and demolition tasks in Falklands because of its recent and very considerable experience in Northern Ireland.

The first operation in which the SAS became involved

*SAS trooper on Fortuna Glacier, South Georgia, April 1982. He wears a white nylon cover over his uniform to provide camouflage. Mittens are essential to prevent frostbite. The furniture on his 5.56mm M16 assault rifle is coloured white to blend in with the terrain.*

was on South Georgia, whose recapture was code-named Operation 'Paraquet'. It is located some 1400km (870 miles) to the southeast of the Falklands, and is even more inhospitable than the Falklands, with genuinely Antarctic weather conditions and a completely mountainous terrain covered by glaciers. The British Government had decided that taking the island would be an excellent way of demonstrating to Argentina that the UK was prepared to use force to regain all her occupied possessions.

The small task force expected to recapture South Georgia comprised the destroyer *Antrim*, the frigate *Plymouth*, the ice patrol ship *Endurance* and the tanker *Tidespring*. The flotilla, designated Task Force 319.9, was under the command of the *Antrim*'s Captain B.C. Young. At Ascension Island, in the middle of the Atlantic Ocean off West Africa, where the task force gathered before the final stage of its approach to the Falkland Islands, the group was joined by the fleet auxiliary *Fort Austin* carrying D Squadron of the SAS. Other elements involved in the operation were Special Boat Service (SBS) personnel and M Company of the Royal Marines' 42 Commando.

In the operations room established on *Antrim*, there soon emerged a number of hot debates about the optimum method of retaking South Georgia. Major Cedric Delves, the commander of D Squadron, was particularly keen for his men to have the leading role. Some of his proposals underestimated the acute difficulties of the weather conditions on South Georgia, but agreement was finally reached for the squadron's Mountain Troop to be landed by helicopter on Fortuna Glacier, and then move on foot to establish a number of observation posts (OPs) around the main Argentinian positions at Leith and Grytviken.

The move to recapture South Georgia was bloodless, but plagued by bad luck and bad weather. The first mission on 21 April was abandoned because of the appalling weather, and two Wessex helicopters crashed while extracting the troopers, fortunately without loss of life.

Undeterred by this setback, however, Delves tried a seaborne approach. On 3 April, therefore, the squadron's Boat Troop, using Gemini inflatables, tried to establish positions on Grass Island. Two of the craft broke down and were swept away by heavy winds, although the crews of both were later rescued. All thoughts of taking the island were temporarily put aside as news reached the British flotilla that an

Argentinian submarine was approaching. The ships scattered, bringing to an end the SAS's so far unsuccessful effort to retake South Georgia.

On 25 April, *Antrim*, *Plymouth* and newly arrived frigate *Brilliant* combined for a daring raid on Grytviken. Single troops of Royal Marines, SBS and SAS were assembled for a helicopter assault on the settlement. While *Antrim* and *Plymouth* bombarded the shore, the men were landed and moved towards the positions held by the Argentinians, who were at a loss about how to counter this move. As the Argentinians considered a call for their surrender, *Antrim* sailed into the bay with orders to level the settlement's buildings if the enemy decided to fight. This proved unnecessary, however, as the Argentinians surrendered without the British troops firing a shot.

## INFILTRATING THE FALKLANDS

The recapture of the Falklands was not fated to be so easy, but the campaign offered the SAS Regiment an excellent chance to display its wide range of military skills. But before any British landing could take place, the numerical strength, composition, morale and disposition of the Argentinian forces had to be discovered, and this required the insertion onto the islands of small SAS teams to reconnoitre enemy positions.

First to land were the men of G Squadron, who were flown in with members of the SBS by Royal Navy Sea

### SIR MICHAEL ROSE

Commanding officer of 22 SAS Regiment during the Falklands War in 1982, Lieutenant-Colonel Michael Rose was largely responsible with Brigadier Peter de la Billière for the highly active part played by the Regiment in the course of the British operation to retake the Falkland Islands. As soon as he heard of the Argentine invasion of the islands, Rose lobbied Brigadier Julian Thompson, commander of 3 Commando Brigade, Royal Marines, for inclusion of the SAS in the Landing Force Task Group. Towards the end of the campaign, Rose and Rod Bell, a Royal Marines officer fluent in Spanish, conducted psychological warfare operations by radio against the Argentine headquarters at Port Stanley, highlighting the Argentines' weak position and hopeless situation. This speeded the collapse of the Argentine resistance effort, and on the afternoon of 14 June Rose flew into Stanley by helicopter to start the talks that led to the formal surrender of General Mario Menendez and his forces. Rose later commanded the UN forces in Bosnia with the rank of lieutenant-general, and was later knighted for his excellent work.

*BELOW: Disaster on Fortuna Glacier. A Wessex helicopter lies wrecked during the attempt to rescue D Squadron's Mountain Troop before the SAS soldiers froze to death.*

*ABOVE: The Argentine submarine* Santa Fe *lies in Grytviken harbour, disabled after a helicopter attack. The SAS, SBS and Royal Navy cooperated closely during the capture of Grytviken.*

*BELOW: The terrain around Grytviken. The scratch force which seized it comprised two SAS troops, some SBS soldiers and a handful of Royal Marines – only 70 men in total.*

King helicopters flown from the carrier *Hermes*, plans for a HALO jump onto the southern tip of West Falkland having been abandoned. In the fashion typical of SAS operations, the men were loaded down with equipment and weapons: 'Our bergens were packed to the brim with everything from waterproofs to quilted over-trousers, rations, communications equipment and ammunition. Everyone carried a LAW [US-made 66mm Light Anti-tank Weapon]. They were flavour of the month, being light but packing a powerful punch, and once you'd used it you could throw it away. Other kit included mini-torches, a change of clothing, gloves, woolly hat, sleeping bag and a bivi-bag which completely protected your "slug" (sleeping bag) from rain and sleet.'

One of the main tasks that Rear Admiral John Woodward, the commander of the Carrier Battle Group, earmarked for the early part of the campaign was the 'softening up' of Argentine positions on the islands by a combination of air attack and shore bombardment. At the same time, possible landing sites were surveyed by SAS and SBS teams, whose activities in this regard started during May.

'The insertion was to be carried out under the overall direction of the carrier *Hermes*. We were the first wave and would be landed on East Falkland under the

cover of darkness (fortunately the pilots had night vision goggles to aid their approach). I remember the helicopter crewman looking at me with a look of total disbelief on his face as we loaded the bergens, he thought they were too heavy to lift, let alone carry across the island.

'Our hands and faces were heavily cammed up as we sped across the water in the Sea King towards our drop-off point. Inside the fuselage it was totally dark, apart from the reflection of the navigation lights on the pilots' control panel. The plan was for us to leave the aircraft as quickly as possible when it touched down, both to give us more chance of remaining undetected and to make the helicopter's journey back safer ... To this end the bergens had been stashed in such a way that they could be pulled out by the last two who left the aircraft.

## LYING-UP

'Then we were over land and the signal was given to prepare for landing. The helicopter touched down and we were out into the cold night. We moved like lightning and the gear was off in no time. The crewman patted my arm and I saw him give me the thumbs up to wish me good luck, then he and the aircraft were gone. Then we were off, heading at speed away from

*ABOVE: The Task Force sails towards the Falklands after the retaking of South Georgia. It was the SAS's job to get its men onto the islands to recce possible landing sites before the main landings.*

the landing site (LS) in case the Argies had a fix on us and sprung an ambush. The rain started to lash down as we began our journey. We must have looked like a bunch of trolls, what with our heavy bergens, windproof smocks, webbing and waterproof gaiters to keep the wet off our ankles. After a while we made a quick stop to check our position before moving off again.

'After two hours' marching we stopped and found a lying-up position (LUP). We couldn't go any farther because dawn was approaching and we risked being caught if we didn't go to ground. So we had to waste a day lying around doing nothing.

'The next night we set off again and quickly reached our target area and established a LUP and a forward OP, which was manned by two men during the day, while the other two would man the main "hide", ready to give covering fire it the OP was compromised. It was bloody freezing all the time, but especially at night, and the ground was so wet that it managed to soak everything through. As a result, it was impossible to be comfortable, and so the whole time was spent operating in an unending gloom.'

*ABOVE: A Sea King helicopter – the type used to transport D Squadron to Pebble Island on the night of 14/15 May to attack the Argentine airfield on the island.*

The SAS undertook many observation missions during the Falklands campaign, and typical of these was a four-man patrol commanded by Captain Aldwin Wight of G Squadron. The team was landed on East Falkland at the end of April with the job of observing Argentine movements in and around Stanley. The patrol established a 'hide' on Beaver Ridge overlooking the town and started to report on Argentine activity. The patrol also saw that the Argentinians had a helicopter night dispersal area between Mount Kent and

Mount Estancia. Receiving this report, the Task Force sent in a pair of Harrier warplanes to find and destroy it: the result was the destruction of three Argentine helicopters. Wight's patrol remained out for 26 days before being relieved on 25 May.

## FIREPOWER AND KIT

A factor that emerges as a major aspect of SAS operations in the Falklands is the very great weight of the loads that the men carried: 'In the Falklands it was a question of guys carrying vast amounts of everything. But there was never enough room in your bergen or in your webbing and so there had to be a compromise. No one carried enough food, in the sense of keeping you well-fed, so a lot of the guys smoked because cigarettes dulled the appetite and were lighter to carry than rations.

'As far as weapons were concerned, it all depended on the task in hand. I remember one short-term job which involved observing the enemy where there was a patrol mix of M16, SLR, Colt Commando and GPMG. Each one of us also had a 9mm Browning High Power and as many Claymore mines and LAWs as could be carried. Each of us ended up humping around some 60kg of kit in total, which is bloody torture. I was carrying three types of ammunition: 9mm for the pistol, 5.56mm for my M16 (I had six fully loaded mags on me plus the one in the weapon) and

*LEFT: The aftermath of the SAS's raid on Pebble Island. A total of 11 Argentinian aircraft were destroyed during the action, with the Regiment suffering only two minor injuries.*

around 1000 7.62mm rounds for the GPMG. In addition to clothing, rations and ammunition, every patrol also had to carry a radio and spare batteries.

'The ironic thing about the ammo is that we rarely used it, and we prayed that we wouldn't have to. The last thing we wanted was the Argies to spot us. All we wanted to do was go out, do our observing and then come back unscathed. In reality, if you had to fight your way out of a situation it meant you had let the opposition know you were there ... Having said that, in the back of your mind it was always satisfying to know that if you were compromised, you had enough firepower to give the enemy hell for up to three quarters of an hour.'

The Argentinians had 11,000 men and 42 aircraft on the Falklands, but despite this fact the SAS soldiers (and the SBS for that matter) found themselves in the position to insert teams with impunity. With a terrible irony, indeed, the heaviest casualties suffered by the SAS during the campaign took place during a crossdecking exercise from *Hermes* to the assault ship *Intrepid*. As the light started to fade on 19 May, one last journey was undertaken by the Sea King helicopter with men from D and G Squadrons in its hold. As the helicopter made one last circuit around *Intrepid* while her flightdeck was cleared of another aircraft, what was probably a giant petrel hit the engine and caused the helicopter to pitch into the sea with the loss of 20 men including 18 SAS soldiers. This was the Regiment's highest single loss since World War II.

One of the most interesting of the SAS's operations in the Falklands campaign took place not on East Falkland, the location of the war's major fighting, bit on Pebble Island off the northern coast of West Falkland. Immediately after their seizure of the islands, the Argentinians had created an airstrip and based on it a number of Pucara light attack aircraft that could have posed a major threat to British ground forces once they had landed on East Falkland. The SAS was thus allocated the task of eliminating these warplanes, with naval support provided by the carrier *Hermes*, the destroyer *Broadsword* for the air defence of the *Hermes*, and the destroyer *Glamorgan* for shore bombardment.

### SHOOTING UP PEBBLE ISLAND

The raid proper was prefaced by a reconnaissance of the airstrip by men of D Squadron's Boat Troop, who landed on the island by canoe. The SAS had at first been instructed to destroy the aircraft, their ground crews and the island's garrison. Strong headwinds, meant that *Hermes* took longer than expected to reaching the flying-off point, and the SAS had only 30 rather than the original 90 minutes to carry out its tasks, as the helicopters which would insert and extract the assault team had to be back on board the *Hermes* before daybreak. In the shortened time available to the troops, the aircraft therefore became the priority targets.

*This Fijian SAS trooper of the Falklands War wears a Gore-tex jacket. This breathable material allows the exit but not the entry of moisture. Unusually, he carries an SLR in favour of the lighter and smaller-calibre M16.*

## CEDRIC DELVES

Major Cedric Delves was the popular and extremely successful commanding officer of D Squadron during the operations to recapture the Falkland Islands in 1982. Delves was awarded a DSO for his actions in the conflict, which included masterminding and accepting the Argentine surrender on South Georgia (22 April), leading the daring raid on Pebble Island (14-15 May) that destroyed all Argentine air capability in this location. He also coordinated a diversionary attack against Darwin (21 May) to draw off Argentine attention and forces before the main landings around San Carlos Water farther to the northwest, and oversaw SAS missions in the area to the west of Stanley on East Falkland in the period leading up to the Argentine surrender.

During the night of 14 May, Sea King helicopters of 846 Squadron took off from *Hermes* with 45 members of D Squadron on board. The helicopters landed some 6km (3.7 miles) from the enemy airstrip on Pebble Island. The squadron's Mountain Troop was tasked with the destruction of the Argentine aircraft, while the other two troops sealed off the approaches to the airstrip and formed a ready reserve. As the party moved off, over 100 81mm mortar bombs, explosive charges and 66mm LAW rockets were unloaded from the helicopters.

The SAS party, each man carrying two mortar bombs, was guided to the target by a member of the Boat Troop, while other men of the troop constituted a protective screen for the mortar team. 'I waited with the cut-off group before joining the killer group.

Mountain Troop went forward, but then we spotted an enemy sentry and everyone froze. My heart started pounding and I tightened the grip on my M16. Instinctively, I slipped off the safety catch. We thought we had been spotted, but our luck was in, he didn't see us. We crept onto the airfield and laid charges on seven of the aircraft. Moments later the place erupted as we opened up with our small arms and LAWs. Using three-round bursts, I emptied a magazine into a Pucara, the bullets sending shards of Perspex into the air.

'To my left a 66mm rocket slammed into the side of another Pucara, engulfing it in a fireball. The crackle of small-arms fire filled the air as the explosive charges started to detonate. I clipped a fresh mag into my M16 and looked around for fresh targets. By this time all the aircraft were either burning or had been riddled with bullets, their undercarriages shot away and their fuselages full of holes. In the background I heard the crump of artillery shells exploding as Glamorgan fired high explosive rounds into the enemy's ammunition dump and fuel stores. The opposition was nowhere to be seen. This is too good to be true, I thought.

'Then the raiding party and the cut-off team regrouped and prepared to move out. Just before we did, we received enemy small-arms fire. One of our boys went down. Instinctively we returned a hail of fire, each man firing controlled bursts from his weapon. Those who had M203s fired grenades at the Argies. It did the trick because we received no more hostile fire.

*BELOW: Typical Falklands terrain. For individual SAS soldiers, lying in an OP meant living in the cold, wet soil for up to four weeks at a time collecting intelligence on the enemy.*

*ABOVE: SAS troops on East Falkland after the British landings at San Carlos on 21 May. For the last part of the campaign the Regiment had B, D and G Squadrons on the islands.*

We continued to fall back, more quickly now lest the enemy were regrouping for another go. The wounded man was grabbed and hauled along (we never leave our wounded behind, it's an unwritten law in the Regiment).

'We bugged out at speed, reaching the landing site to await our lift back to *Hermes*. Bang on time the choppers came in, and a happy D Squadron was lifted out. I for one had expected a heavy firefight when we got to the airfield, but it never materialised. We could have hit the garrison if we had had more time, but as it was we all felt pleased with ourselves.'

As the SAS party pulled back, six Pucaras, four Turbo-Mentor armed trainer and counter-insurgency aircraft and one Skyvan utility transport lay wrecked on the grass. The SAS party had also destroyed a large quantity of Argentine ammunition, and also denied the Argentinians further use of the airstrip.

The raid on Pebble Island was a classic SAS action, highly reminiscent of the type of operation undertaken by the Regiment in World War II.

As the Task Force prepared for the main landings around San Carlos Water, the SAS and SBS were given a more offensive role in the form of diversionary attacks on the Argentinians. One of these was conducted in the area of Darwin and Goose Green by 40 men of D Squadron under Major Delves.

'Heavily outnumbered, the SAS convinced the Argentine garrison that they were under attack by a whole battalion. Return fire was wild and inaccurate and by dawn the 40-man team was heading towards San Carlos water.'

The British plan was to establish a strong beachhead at San Carlos and then strike across East Falkland to Stanley, the capital. The days and weeks after the landings found the SAS and SBS in support of the conventional units with probing missions to locate enemy forward positions. Late in May, for example, men of the SAS Regiment seized Mount Kent and held it before being reinforced by 42 Commando, and early in June five SAS teams were landed on West Falkland. In one of the last actions of the war, a combined SAS and SBS force launched a diversionary raid opposite Stanley on the night of 13/14 June to take pressure off 2 Para's attack on Wireless Ridge. Despite an intense barrage of enemy fire, only three of the British raiders were injured before they were forced to retire. The next day a ceasefire was agreed, bringing the war to an end.

More than anything else, however, it had been the intelligence that individual SAS teams had relayed back to the fleet in the weeks before the landings that had been the regiment's most valuable contribution to the eventual British victory.

# CHAPTER 7

# THE GULF WAR

## During the Gulf War of 1991, the SAS scoured the deserts of Iraq for Scud missile-launch sites, the continued use of which not only threatened lives, but also the survival of the alliance fighting Iraq.

On 2 August 1990 about 100,000 Iraqi troops, with six divisions of the elite Republican Guard in the van, invaded Kuwait, its southern and very much smaller neighbour. The Kuwaiti armed forces were able to offer only limited and short-term resistance, and within a few hours the Iraqi dictator, Saddam Hussein, had achieved his object of seizing the tiny oil-rich state, which would allow an expansion of Iraq's very short coastline and permit the looting of Kuwait's considerable financial resources. Soon political outrage in the United Nations (UN) led to a

*ABOVE: An SAS soldier at the Regiment's base at Al Jouf in Saudi Arabia just before the opening of hostilities against Iraq in mid-January 1991. The base was ideally located to get patrols into Iraq.*

*LEFT: Sergeant Andy McNab with the bergen he carried on his back during his patrol behind Iraqi lines. When he and his men were discovered, they ditched their packs and made a run for Syria.*

great build-up of personnel and material in Saudi Arabia as an alliance of Western and Middle Eastern nations launched a military operation to expel the Iraqis from Kuwait.

As troops and equipment for the American-led UN force began to flood into Saudi Arabia by air and sea, US and British special forces units were also deployed, the latter including elements of the SAS Regiment.

The Gulf War, as it came to be called, saw the greatest concentration of SAS troops in an operational theatre since World War II. The men of the Regiment were originally tasked with the exceptionally difficult job of rescuing British citizens held as hostages by the Iraqis. Some 800 Britons in Kuwait and another 1000 in Iraq were under threat of death, held as 'human shields' around vital Iraqi military, government and industrial targets, whose loss to allied air attack would otherwise have severely damaged Iraq's ability to wage the inevitable war.

With hindsight, the task of rescuing the hostages would have clearly been impossible, for these men, women and children had been scattered to many locations all over Iraq, making the establishment of their whereabouts, let alone their simultaneous rescues, impossible by any rational thinking. Although the SAS would have used all its resources, both human and technical, in the task of trying to reach as many hostages as possible, many more would in all probability have been killed by their Iraqi guards at the first suggestion of a rescue effort, and others would probably have been killed as they were evacuated across the desert. For all concerned, therefore, it was fortunate that matters did not come to this because Saddam Hussein, in a rare moment of humanity, or more probably political pragmatism, let most of the hostages go before the outbreak of hostilities with the Allies.

*ABOVE: Iraqi Scud surface-to-surface missiles, which Saddam Hussein used in an effort to bring Israel into the war, which would have certainly split the UN Coalition.*

## OPERATIONAL BACKGROUND

In 1990, a virtually bankrupt Iraq seized Kuwait and all its assets, both financial and natural. The United Nations organised a huge military effort to wrest Kuwait back from its invaders by use of high-quality armed forces from an alliance based mainly in Saudi Arabia. The main threat to the unity of the alliance was the Iraqi use of Scud missiles against Israel. Saddam Hussein hoped to prick the neutral Jewish state into the type of retaliation that might have caused the disintegration of the alliance: anti-Israeli Arab states may have demanded the evacuation of Saudi Arabia by pro-Israeli states. The SAS and American special forces were instrumental in blunting this dangerous Iraqi tactic.

The Americans had also considered a similar type of operation with their own special forces. Fortunately, the resolution of the problem by Saddam himself meant that the US and British elite units could now concentrate their efforts on other tasks offering a greater chance of success. All special forces elements in the Gulf region were under the control of the Special Operations Command of Central Command (SOCCENT), which was an Allied organisation coordinated by the Americans.

### FIRST DEPLOYMENT

In August 1990, D and G Squadrons of 22 SAS were present in the Gulf region, and using their time profitably in the perfection of their desert warfare skills. One of those SAS soldiers remembers the rapid build-up in Saudi Arabia: 'We had been operating in Oman with a batch of new four-wheel drive vehicles called Light Strike Vehicles (LSVs), which were designed specifically for rough terrain. We had spent weeks putting them through a series of punishing tests. They were good, though the suspension couldn't survive a drop from a Chinook helicopter from an altitude of 100m, which we discovered when one was accidentally dropped. Still, there isn't much kit that can survive that sort of treatment. We were thoroughly acclimatised by the time we touched down in Saudi, though none of us were prepared for the piss-poor weather we would encounter later on operations.

'So there we were, a motley crew with bergens and weapons walking across the tarmac to a group of waiting trucks. Around us, an army of multi-national air force personnel worked feverishly on their aircraft. We didn't know what the high command had in store for us, so all we could do was train for any likely operation that might crop up. By late December 1990, the majority of the Regiment had been deployed to the Gulf, including some blokes from R Squadron, the reserve. However, because no specific role had been assigned to us, patience began to wear a little thin.'

The British special forces group in the Gulf finally numbered some 700 men, and included elements of the Special Boat Service (SBS) and RAF special forces aircrew. Of this total, the SAS contributed 300 men in the forms of A, B, D and G Squadrons and 15 men of R Squadron (G Squadron was not used in the end).

Even though the build-up of American and British forces in Saudi Arabia was rapid, opening the possibility of their extensive use well before the main ground forces were ready for offensive action, the high command seemed to have no task for them in the short term except for a number of 'penny packet' operations. This was because General Norman Schwarzkopf, the Allied commander, had gained a poor impression of special forces in Vietnam and still harboured considerable distrust about them. General Sir Peter de la Billière, the ex-SAS commander of the British forces in Saudi Arabia, certainly thought so: 'At first Norman Schwarzkopf had opposed the idea of deploying (spe-

cial forces) behind enemy lines, on the grounds that there was no task which could not be carried out by the Allies' overwhelming air power or, later, by the conventional armoured forces. I myself was not prepared to recommend special operations unless two conditions were fulfilled: one was that there must be a real, worthwhile role for the SAS to perform, and the other that we must have some means of extricating our men in an emergency.'

Peter de la Billière finally succeeded in persuading Schwarzkopf that the special forces should be given a chance to prove themselves. The task now was to find a worthwhile mission for them to undertake.

## GROUNDING THE MISSILES

The solution became apparent on 18 January 1991, when Iraq launched its first Scud surface-to-surface missile against Israel in a cleverly conceived effort to bring the Jewish state into the war on the Allied side, and thus alienate Arab states, such as Egypt and Saudi Arabia, then staunch members of the alliance.

The Scud is an elderly, obsolescent and basic weapon of its type. Powered by a solid-propellant

*BELOW: As well as the SAS, the Americans deployed their elite teams to the Gulf to fight the Iraqis. This is a Delta Force Fast Attack Vehicle, which Delta used to hunt for Scuds inside Iraq.*

rocket and carrying a high-explosive warhead that can, however, be replaced by a warhead filled with biological or chemical warfare agents, the missile is fired in the general direction of the target and is not notable for its accuracy, especially in the extended-range versions developed by the Iraqis themselves from the basic Soviet weapon. The missile is aided in its tactical deployment by the fact that it can be launched from fixed sites or, more importantly as the campaign developed, mobile launchers.

The main threat of the Scud was not the direct damage that it could cause, even though this could have been great if biological or chemical warheads had been landed in a heavily populated area, but the indirect damage of spurring Israeli retaliation.

The possibility of a disaster resulting from Israeli retaliation was therefore very real, and special forces units were thus allocated the responsibility of finding the Iraqis' mobile launchers and fixed sites, and then either destroying them or calling in air strikes to achieve the same end.

On 19 January, the SAS moved up to its Forward Operating Base (FOB), one day's drive away from the

*ABOVE: The SAS patrol codenamed 'Bravo Two Zero' just prior to being inserted into Iraq, whose exploits became famous thanks to the book of the same name published after the war.*

border of western Iraq. The whole operation that was about to be launched was very much a joint undertaking between US special forces and the SAS, and had two primary objectives: the tracking down and destruction of the static and mobile Scud missiles, and the location and destruction of Iraq's concealed communications network, whose construction Saddam had supervised over a period of several years on the urging of Western defence and intelligence agencies, which had succeeded in impressing on the Iraqi leader the paramount importance of a nation-wide communications network that was both secure and survivable. This network was based mainly on a series of microwave links via communications towers, and on fibre-optic cables under the ground.

## SCUD HUNTING

The SAS used two methods in its battle against the Scud missile: the installation of static road watch patrols and the implementation of mobile fighting columns. The road watches were risky: eight-man teams were inserted by helicopter up to 300km (186 miles) behind the Iraqi lines to set up covert observation posts (OPs) that kept a watch on the relevant road for any Iraqi activity; if they spotted any worthwhile targets, they called in an air attack. The men had nothing but their legs for movement, and if compromised possessed nothing but their own resources and skills to escape to friendly lines.

In general, the fighting columns each consisted of about 12 heavily armed Land Rover vehicles organised into hunter-killer groups. These columns operated mostly in the 'Scud Box', an area of some 500 square kilometres (195 square miles) near the Iraqi frontier with Jordan. This region included the highway between Baghdad and Amman, the Iraqi and Jordanian capitals respectively, and was usually filled with nomadic Bedouins, civilian traffic and a considerable military presence.

It had at first been planned that this would be the operational area of the LSVs, but events forced a different turn: 'The four two-man LSVs ferried across from Oman were considered ideal for cross-border raids. They had many clever design features, including armoured seats and self-sealing fuel tanks to counter fragmentation damage. But as the Gulf situation escalated, it became clear that instead of operating on a limited scale using the two strike vehicles, the Regiment would be called upon to mount much bigger vehicle-based operations. In the event, LSVs were used by SAS patrols to monitor Iraqi movements, but they didn't cross the border into enemy territory.

'A fleet of new Land Rovers arrived for us from the UK, all stripped down for desert operations and decorated with a host of weapon mounts and additional fittings, including Southdown Protection Systems, which stopped the transmission systems from being damaged on rocks.'

## ROAD WATCH PATROLS

The road watch patrols were the responsibility of B Squadron along three highways in the valley of the River Euphrates, and these patrols constituted the North, Central and South Road Watches. From the very beginning of his operation, the commander of the South Road Watch realised that his position was untenable, so he abandoned it and returned to base, as he was fortunate enough to have a helicopter evacuation capability. The Central Road Watch was just as precarious, so its commander also opted to evacuate his team, although not until after he had called in an air attack on two nearby Iraqi mobile radar systems. Only then did the SAS soldiers depart at high speed, covering some 220km (137 miles) over four extremely cold nights on their trip back to Saudi Arabia.

*BELOW: An RAF special forces Chinook helicopter, which was used to transport SAS patrols into Iraq. For the pilots, these missions involved flying nap-of-the-earth to avoid anti-aircraft weapons.*

*ABOVE: From 20 January 1991, the SAS sent heavily armed Land Rover patrols into Iraq to search for Iraqi mobile Scud teams. These patrols consisted of 12 Land Rovers each.*

The account of the North Road Watch is a combination of heroism and tragedy. Delivered 300km (186 miles) from the nearest Allied outpost, the men quickly settled down to the OP routine of keeping watch, sleeping, the type of minor duties that kept their minds alert. On the second day of the operation the team saw the arrival of an Iraqi convoy; it halted quite close to, indeed right on top of, the SAS position. The British soldiers were then somewhat worried that the convoy was in fact a mobile anti-aircraft battery, with the relevant guns and radar equipment. The inevitable soon took place, for the Iraqis discovered the SAS team's position through the agency not of the Iraqi troops themselves, it might be added, but by a party of civilians attached to the battery. The SAS men had no option but to run for it: carrying their heavy bergens on their backs, they made off with all speed, but almost immediately came under heavy fire from the now thoroughly alerted Iraqi troops, who also brought their anti-aircraft guns into play. One SAS trooper had his bergen literally ripped to shreds by

machine-gun fire: dropping their bergens, the SAS men increased their speed.

It was too far and too obvious to make for Saudi Arabia, so the men made for the closer and less obvious frontier with Syria. In their wake the country was now swarming with troops as the Iraqis determined to catch the enemy party that had been discovered right in their midst. The desert of the Arabian peninsula and the region to its north is wholly inhospitable at the best of times, but in January 1991 it was at the worst of times and the weather was truly appalling, with a mix of rain, sleet, wind and snow. Thus the SAS troopers had to contend not only with the Iraqis but also with the terrain and weather.

The team split to increase its overall chances of evasion, but with little in the way of supplies and the enemy snapping at their heels, the men were forced to maintain a rapid and increasingly tiring pace that inevitably began to take its toll. Sergeant Vince Phillips became detached from his group in the driving sleet and died of a combination of exhaustion and hypothermia in the Iraqi hills, while another member of his three-man group was surrounded by Iraqi soldiers and forced to surrender. Corporal Chris Ryan, the third man of the group, displayed the tenacity and cunning that are more often typical of fiction than fact. Moving by day and night, avoiding all contact, and resting and/or eating wherever he could, this man walked 200km (124 miles) to the Syrian border – an extraordinary achievement made that much more remarkable by the fact that for the last two days he had no water.

The other five men were lucky at first. They reached Al Qaim, a town close to the Jordanian border, before they were encountered by a group of Iraqi soldiers. There followed a firefight in which the outnumbered SAS men held their own because of their better weapons skills, but could not lose the Iraqis despite inflicting severe losses on them. Trooper Robert Consiglio, who was bringing up the rear to cover the group's withdrawal, was hit and killed, and two other men were captured soon after this.

Despite their total exhaustion, the two surviving members of the group pushed ahead. It was an impossible task, and in the face of continued pursuit and dismal weather they approached the limits of their endurance. Almost beyond credibility, they continued to head for the safety of a neutral country, but found it impossible: Lance-Corporal Lane was almost unconscious as his comrade managed to get him into a hut,

*ABOVE: The SAS fighting columns were provided with motorcycle outriders, whose job was to scout ahead and to the flanks of the main column, and pass messages between the vehicles.*

but then died of hypothermia. His companion attempted to escape but was captured.

So ended the road watch venture; with hindsight it is possible to see that the plan was probably a little too audacious. But for the SAS the war was not over: the fighting columns were about to begin.

## SAS FIGHTING COLUMNS

The first of the fighting columns, a line of heavily armed vehicles manned by men of A Squadron, crossed the frontier from Saudi Arabia on 20 January. The vehicles and men were fearsomely armed, but perhaps the most important pieces of kit carried by the column were the Magellan Global Positioning System (GPS) receivers: 'Before the war we had been exercising and using the GPS with great results. In the Gulf smaller sets were available, and their accuracy

*BELOW: One of A Squadron's Land Rovers in western Iraq in late January 1991. Festooned with spare rations, fuel, water and ammunition, they carried anti-tank and anti-aircraft weapons.*

### SIR PETER DE LA BILLIÈRE

A talented, hard-working and courageous man, de la Billière was originally commissioned into the Durham Light Infantry and joined the SAS as a captain in Malaya during 1955. In a distinguished career, he has served with the SAS in Oman, where he took part in the celebrated assault on Jebel Akhdar, and in Aden, where he established a Close Quarter Battle course for troopers engaged in 'Keeni Meeni' operations in 1964. After service in Borneo, de la Billière was the commanding officer of 22 SAS Regiment (1972-4) and, four years later, was appointed Director of the SAS and Commander of the SAS Group. A highly decorated officer, he was responsible for turning the SAS Regiment into a highly capable counter-terrorist unit. The culmination of de la Billière's career was as commander of the British forces sent to the Persian Gulf in 1990 as part of the United Nations alliance against Iraq. Lieutenant-General de la Billière rapidly established a close working relationship with General Norman Schwarzkopf, and the stunning success of the ground offensive in February 1991 owed much to this partnership.

was astonishing. Though they were expensive, for us the GPS receivers were among the best items of kit purchased by the Ministry of Defence. They were brilliant for coordinating rendezvous sites and directing air strikes.'

Some of the dress worn by SAS soldiers in the Gulf campaign differed little from that worn 50 years earlier by SAS men in the desert of North Africa: 'The shemagh, an Arab headdress, was the order of the day. We looked a bit like a bunch of Lawrence of Arabia stand-ins, but they kept the sand and dust out of our faces and that was all that mattered. By mid-January 1991, we were across the border and operating in the Iraqi desert, experiencing the cold nights and savage winds. Desert combats were worn, but on their own were no match for the terrible conditions. So, Goretex jackets, climbing jumpers, gloves, arctic smocks and woolly hats were pulled out of our bergens for warmth. Forget the idea of a smartly dressed patrol, we looked like a bunch of unshaven gypsies.'

Another two columns, in this instance manned by personnel of D Squadron, also entered Iraqi territory to hunt for Scud missiles. The men were not disappointed in this task, for nine days after crossing the border an SAS column came across a camouflaged site from which the Iraqis were preparing to launch Scud missiles against Israel. The SAS commander quickly called in an air attack, and a few minutes elapsed before American F-15 Eagle multi-role warplanes destroyed the missile site. The special forces were beginning to pay back the faith that had been put in them in a big way.

*BELOW: An SAS column behind the lines in Iraq. The Regiment didn't have it all its own way. On 19 February, for example, an SAS patrol was beaten off by the Iraqis near Nukhayb.*

*ABOVE: As well as the vehicle patrols operating in western Iraq, the SAS also fielded a number of foot patrols. They were used to pinpoint Iraqi targets for Allied ground-attack aircraft.*

The mobile columns faced their own dangers, however, and the men had to maintain constant vigilance. During rest and maintenance periods, invariably during daylight hours, the vehicles were always arranged in a defensive circle as a precaution against any Iraqi attack like the one which happened on the same day that the first missile site was 'taken out'. Iraqi vehicles stumbled across an SAS column and engaged it with small arms and heavy machine-gun fire. The men of the column returned the fire without delay and a sharp firefight followed, the men with the stronger nerves and steadier eyes winning: the Iraqis fell back after losing three vehicles and 10 men.

## SCUD ALLEY

The SAS's favourite hunting ground in this campaign was Wadi Amij, otherwise known as 'Scud Alley', near the town of Ar Rutbah. On 3 February, a fighting column from D Squadron located a Scud convoy of 14 vehicles in 'Scud Alley'. The commander called in the request for an air attack, and the SAS men watched as

A-10 and F-15 warplanes shattered the Iraqi convoy with rockets and bombs: one 'Scud'-laden trailer took a direct hit, the entire vehicle being hurled into the air in a huge fireball of burning explosive and petrol; a truck was cast onto its side; and an armoured personnel carrier was punctured by fragments that killed all those inside. Even so, it was clear that the aircraft had not done the whole job, for some of the Iraqi vehicles were still operable.

The SAS column accordingly opened up with its Milan anti-tank missiles, which soon began to find their targets. The Iraqis now realised that they faced a ground as well as aerial opponent, and returned fire with small arms and anti-aircraft guns. Rather than risk heavy casualties when his column was still in the early days of its mission, the SAS commander gave the order for a short withdrawal even as he called for another air attack. As they made off, the men of the SAS heard the sounds of another rocket and bomb attack on the hapless Iraqi convoy.

Not all the engagements between the Scud convoys and the SAS took place in 'Scud Alley'. SAS fighting columns were sometimes reinforced by men flown in by helicopter, often a risky operation.

The men of the SAS also struck at the Iraqi communications network. In the aftermath of one such attack an A Squadron column became involved in running action with an Iraqi force. The SAS troopers succeeded in driving off the Iraqis with Milan and Browning fire. In this way the SAS Regiment made another major contribution to the war against Saddam.

One little known element of the SAS effort in the Gulf War was the collation of intelligence gained from Kuwaiti sources. In Riyadh, the Saudi Arabian capital, several SAS soldiers worked alongside US intelligence personnel to produce detailed information about the strength of the Iraqi forces in Kuwait. The operation involved three SAS linguists, who worked with three American counterparts. Their initial task was to locate and secure a source of regular and reliable information inside Kuwait City itself for the provision of accurate intelligence to build the 'big picture'. The SAS struck gold in the form of 'Mohammed', a ham radio operator contacted via a 'third player' in Geneva. 'Mohammed' used a low-pulse radio equipment that was difficult to detect, and provided a mass of highly accurate information.

In the Gulf War, therefore, the SAS was involved mainly in hunting Scud missiles and their launch sites or vehicles, locating and destroying elements of the Iraqi communications network, and providing intelligence for the Allied high command. The success of the SAS is perhaps best attested by the commendation of General Schwarzkopf: 'I wish to officially commend the 22nd Special Air Service (SAS) Regiment for their totally outstanding performance of military operations during Operation Desert Storm ... The performance of the 22nd Special Air Service (SAS) Regiment during Operation Desert Storm was in the highest traditions of the professional military service and in keeping with the proud history and tradition that has been established by that regiment.'

*BELOW: An Iraqi tank burns after being hit by American F-16s, which were called in by an SAS team on the ground. The Regiment's teams were the 'eyes and ears' of the UN in Iraq.*

# CHAPTER 8

# HOSTAGE-RESCUE

## The high-profile rescue in 1980 of innocent hostages held by terrorists in Iran's London Embassy confirmed the SAS as the world's premier anti-terrorist unit, equipped with magnificent skills and weapons.

In 1972 there appeared a decisive moment in the history of the SAS, although this fact was not appreciated then by the Regiment or, for that matter, the British Government. This turning point was the Olympic Games being held at the time in the West German city of Munich. Here security was non-obtrusive, so it was a straightforward task for a terrorist unit from the Palestinian 'Black September' group to seize and eventually murder 11 Israeli athletes as the West Germans tried to

*ABOVE: In the 'Killing House' the SAS uses live ammunition during hostage-rescue simulations. The aim is to make training as near to the real thing as possible – even if it means fatalities.*

*LEFT: A trooper inside the 'Killing House' armed with a Remington 870 shotgun, which is used to blow off door hinges before a team enters a room or building during a hostage rescue.*

rescue them after they had been held hostage by the terrorists for several days. It was a major outrage, and all the more poignant and devastating as it had been played out in front of the world's media, present in large numbers for coverage of the Olympic Games.

For West Germany the event was a nightmare come true: once again Jews had been taken and killed in Germany. As a result of this disaster, however, the West German Federal Republic looked closely into its security needs and then established the GSG 9 unit, which was to become an expert counter-terrorist organisation.

The British Government was one of many other Western governments which also took on board the notions that their countries were also distinctly at risk to the same type of terrorist attack and their capability for effective response in such circumstances was as limited as that of the West German authorities. Several of these governments therefore followed the West German lead and set up specialised counter-terrorist units. In the UK, the decision was taken not to create a new group for this task but to allocate it as an additional responsibility to an existing element of the British Army: the SAS Regiment. In 1973, therefore, the Regiment established a Counter Revolutionary Warfare (CRW) Wing at Stirling Lines.

## COUNTER-REVOLUTIONARY WARFARE

The fact that the task had been allocated to the SAS was not in itself surprising, for the Regiment already possessed a wartime counter-revolutionary and counter-insurgency capability. In Special Air Service terms, this task comprised operations to covertly infiltrate areas by sea, land or air; gathering intelligence about the strength and disposition of hostile guerrilla forces; ambushing and harassing insurgents; undertaking assassination and demolition operations; border surveillance; implementation of a 'hearts and minds' policy; and training and liaising with friendly guerrilla forces. The new brief now appended hostage-rescue to this long list.

At Hereford every member of the Regiment's Sabre Squadrons undertakes the intensive Close-Quarter Battle (CQB) course: for the development and refinement of a high-quality capability in hostage-rescue operations a special building, known as the 'Killing House', was erected. The type of operations and skills practised by members of the Regiment in the 'Killing House' are described by an SAS trooper:

'Inside the "Killing House" live ball ammunition is used all the time, though the walls have a special rubber coating which absorbs the impact of rounds as they hit (and so prevents the likelihood of a ricochet). Before going into any hostage scene, the team always go through the potential risks they may face. The priority is always to eliminate the immediate threat. If you burst into a room and there are three terrorists – one with a knife, one holding a grenade and one pointing a machine gun – you always shoot the one with the gun, as he or she is the immediate threat.

*BELOW: At Stirling Lines, the 'Killing House' is in constant use. This means that at any one time there are between 10 and 20 men practising their hostage-rescue drills in the building.*

'The aim is to double tap [two shots fired in quick succession] the target until he drops. Only head shots count – in a room that can sometimes be filled with smoke there is no room for mistakes. Hits to the arms, legs and body will be discounted; constant drills are required to ensure shooting standards are high. If the front man of the team has a problem with his primary weapon, which is usually a Heckler & Koch MP5 sub-machine gun, he will hold it to his left, drop down on one knee and draw his handgun. The man behind him will then stand over him until the problem with the defective weapon has been rectified. Then the point man will tap his mate's weapon or shout "close", indicating that he is ready to continue with the assault. Two magazines are usually carried on the weapon, but magnetic clips are used as opposed to tape. Though most of the time only one mag is required, having two together is useful because the additional weight can stop the weapon pulling into the air when firing.

## COMBATING TERRORISTS

'The aim is to polish your skills as a team so that everyone is trained up to the same level, thinking on the same wavelength and aware of each other's actions. The "House" is full of corridors, small rooms and obstacles, and often the scenario demands that the rescue be carried out in darkness (a basic SOP [standard operating procedure] on a live mission is for the power to be cut before the team goes into a building to aid the element of surprise). The rooms are pretty barren, but they can be laid out to resemble the size and layout of a potential target, and the hostages will often be mixed in among the gunmen.

'Confidence in using live ammunition is developed by using "live" hostages, who are drawn from the teams (the men wear body armour but no helmets). They usually sit at a table or stand on a marked spot, waiting to be "rescued". The CQB range also includes electronically operated figures that can be controlled by the training staff. At a basic level, for example, three figures will have their backs to you as you enter the room. Suddenly, all three will turn and one will be armed. In that split second you must target the correct "body" – if you don't you will "kill" a hostage and the gunman will "kill" you.

'A variety of situations can be developed by the instructors. For example, they may tell the team leaders to stand down minutes before a rescue drill starts, forcing the team members to go through on their own. Other "funnies" include smoke, gas, obstacles to

*ABOVE: Abseiling equipment is often used by SAS hostage-rescue teams for descending unseen from above to force entries. Much practice is needed to ensure speedy and smooth descents.*

separate team members from their colleagues, as well as loudspeakers to simulate crowd noises and shouting.

'New weapons and ammunition are continually being tested in the "House", and among the latest introductions is a new fragmentation round. It explodes on impact, so if a team has to storm a boat it will hit the bulkheads and burst without ricocheting, unlike ball rounds.

'Speed, fast reactions and slick drills are the key during CQB drills. Four-man assault groups are normally split into two reams of two, and each man is given specific areas inside each room to clear.'

## RESCUE AT MOGADISHU

The development and implementation of the best hostage-rescue tactics could not be rushed, but were pushed forward with all due speed; by the late 1970s the SAS could be confident that it was fully trained in hostage-rescue tactics. The Regiment had approached its new task with its usual combination of cool determination and far-sighted thoroughness. Two of its men, Major Alastair Morrison and Sergeant Barry Davies, had taken part in the dramatic rescue of German hostages by GSG 9 at Mogadishu, the capital of Somalia, in 1977 (see below), and numerous exchange-training exercises had been undertaken with foreign hostage-rescue units, such as the US Army's Delta Force and the French Army's GIGN. The Regiment was confident that it could tackle a hostage-

*ABOVE: The SAS has close links with other hostage-rescue units around the world, such as the American Delta Force above. This is to pool information regarding hardware and tactics.*

rescue scenario successfully, although there inevitably remained an element of doubt as the SAS's training had yet to be put to the practical test. There was, of course, only one method for evaluating the reality and practicality of the SAS's thinking, and that was in a hostage-rescue situation within the UK. But first the Regiment had to assist an ally's hostage-rescue unit.

On 13 October 1977, four Palestinian terrorists hijacked a Boeing Model 737 airliner of the German national airline, Lufthansa, on a flight from the Balearic Islands to Germany. The leader of the terrorist group was Zohair Akache, a notorious terrorist often styling himself 'Captain Mahmoud'. The demands of the hijackers for the release of the airliner, its five crew and 86 passengers were the immediate freedom of 11 members of the Baader-Meinhof terrorist organisation then in West German jails.

After a number of intermediate airport landings and take-offs, the airliner finally arrived at Mogadishu in the Somali Republic. It was followed onto the ground after a comparatively short interval by another German airliner, specifically selected in preference to a military transport for reasons of camouflage, carrying a 30-strong detachment of the GSG 9 organisation under Ulrich Wegener, the unit's commander. In addition, the aircraft carried two members of the SAS Regiment – Major Alastair Morrison and Sergeant Barry Davies – who had brought with them a number of newly developed stun grenades and were ready to give general advice on tactics (in fact, the assault that finally took place was planned by the two Britons).

## AIRCRAFT STORM

On 16 October, 'Captain Mahmoud' murdered the captain of the airliner and threw his body from the aircraft onto the tarmac. Inside the airliner conditions, both moral and physical, were deteriorating rapidly and 'Captain Mahmoud' was becoming increasingly irrational. He set a deadline of 0255 hours on 18 October for the release of all the Baader-Meinhof terrorists, with the threat that he would otherwise blow

*ABOVE: The Italian hostage-rescue unit*, Nucleo Operativo Central di Sicurezza (NOCS), *which the SAS helped to establish in the late 1970s. Today it is one of the world's top anti-terrorist units.*

*BELOW: Germany's crack GSG 9. Formed after the terrorist incident at the 1972 Munich Olympics, it has frequent exchanges with the SAS and other Western counter-terrorist units.*

up the airliner. In concert with the two SAS men, Wegener decided that the time had come for GSG 9 to launch its assault on the airliner to rescue the increasingly threatened hostages.

At 0205 hours Somali soldiers lit a fire on the runway ahead of the airliner as a diversion to attract the attention of the Palestinian terrorists, and two of the hijackers went to the cockpit to assess the fire's significance. At 0207 hours the emergency doors over the airliner's wings and at the front and rear of its fuselage were all blown open by special explosive charges, and stun grenades were thrown into the fuselage. There followed a blinding flash and an extremely loud bang, then the four GSG 9 assault teams, led by Wegener, stormed into the airliner. An intense battle raged for the next five minutes as the West German soldiers encountered and shot each of the terrorists. 'Captain Mahmoud' appeared in the doorway of the flight-deck and was hit by a hail of bullets, but still managed to throw two grenades before he was finally cut down by a burst from a Heckler & Koch MP5 submachine gun. With great good fortune, the grenades he had thrown in his dying moments rolled under some seats and exploded without harming anyone. Wegener himself killed one of the terrorists with a head shot, and the outcome of the battle was three dead terrorists and one wounded survivor, Suhaila Sayeh, the sole woman in the terrorist group. Three hostages had also been hurt, though fortunately none were killed.

### IRANIAN EMBASSY SIEGE

The operation had been a stunning success. The involvement of the SAS was immediately admitted by the British Government. The immediate result for the SAS Regiment  was that each Sabre Squadron undertook CRW training on a rotational basis, thereby ensuring that the UK would have a fully prepared hostage-rescue capability available on a 24-hour basis.

It was May 1980 before the first hostage-rescue situation finally took place on British soil. On the morning of 30 April 1980, six armed terrorists of the Democratic Revolutionary Front for the Liberation of Arabistan, which is a part of Iran populated by ethnic Arabs rather than Iranians, hurled themselves into the Iranian Embassy at No 16 Princes Gate in London and seized 22 hostages. The terrorists were armed with Czech-made Skorpion submachine guns, Belgian Browning semi-automatic handguns and Soviet-made grenades. The terrorists, who were backed by Iraq at a time of steadily deteriorating Iraqi-Iranian relations

that became open war later in the year, demanded the release of 92 Arabs detained in Iranian jails as well as safe passage out of the UK for themselves as soon as their primary demand had been met, and said that they would start killing their hostages if their demands were not met.

Police negotiators began the difficult task of calming the situation and at the same time wearing down the terrorists over the telephone, while, simultaneously, specialist units began to arrive and seal off the immediate area of the situation. These specialist units included police marksmen of the D11 unit, anti-terrorist officers of the C13 unit, the Special Patrol Group, and members of C7, the Metropolitan Police's Technical Support Branch. These were destined to be only supporting actors in the crisis, however, because the central players had yet to arrive.

A Special Projects Team was sent immediately from Hereford,

*This SAS hostage-rescue trooper at the Iranian Embassy in May 1980 is wearing a black Nomex flame-resistant assault suit, Kevlar armour and respirator. His weapon is the Heckler & Koch MP5 submachine gun.*

where there was always one Sabre Squadron, divided into Special Projects Teams, on 24-hour stand-by for the hostage-rescue and anti-terrorist role. This Red Team comprised a captain and 24 troopers of B Squadron. Also at the scene was Lieutenant-Colonel Michael Rose, commander of the Regiment, and it was he who authorised the implementation of an 'immediate action plan' if any short-term threat to the hostages became apparent.

## IMMEDIATE ACTION

As it became clear that an instant rescue attempt could not be undertaken, a 'deliberate assault plan' was created for implementation at the time and spot chosen by the SAS. Red Team was several times put on full alert for a rapid assault when the terrorists made particular threats against the hostages, but these episodes fortunately turned out to be false alarms, though they were extremely fraught for all that. Reinforcements arrived during the afternoon of 2 May in the form of the Blue Team, as negotiations between the police and terrorists continued.

As they were doing so, both SAS assault teams studied every scrap of intelligence that could be garnered about the Iranian Embassy building. Microphones were installed by MI5, the British counter-intelligence organisation now known as the Security Service, in the walls and down the chimneys. This made it possible for the police and SAS to establish with a fair degree of exactitude the location of the terrorists and hostages. At the nearby Regent's Park Barracks, British Army engineers built a full-scale model of the embassy. At government level, Prime Minister Margaret Thatcher discussed the crisis with senior members of the Ministry of Defence, MI5, MI6 (the British military intelligence organisation now known as the Secret Intelligence Service) and the SAS. These meetings, known as the Cabinet Office Briefing Room (COBRA), decided that a programme of caution and patience was the best policy.

Time was nonetheless running out for the authorities, however, for the Government's steadfast refusal to make concessions, combined with the non-appearance of the Arab mediators demanded by the terrorists, caused the situation inside the Iranian Embassy to deteriorate. Ali Mohammed, codenamed 'Salim', the terrorist leader, began to sound increasingly volatile and nervous as he spoke to police negotiators during 5 May. By early in the evening of that day matters had gone seriously wrong, for several gunshots were heard

from inside the Iranian Embassy. Then the body of the embassy's chief press officer, Abbas Lavasani, was thrown out onto the pavement outside the building. Sir David McNee, Commissioner of the Metropolitan Police, telephoned COBRA to inform the authorities that he was entrusting further authority for the situation to the SAS. At 1907 hours Rose formally took control and ordered the implementation of the rescue plan, Operation 'Nimrod'

The assault on the Iranian Embassy and the rescue of the hostages are detailed by men who were involved:

'When we had arrived at the start of the siege, we had been told to be ready to storm the building within 15 minutes. This would mean going in using firearms, stun grenades and CS gas and trying to reach the hostages before they were killed. At that stage we had no idea of the hostages' whereabouts. I looked at the

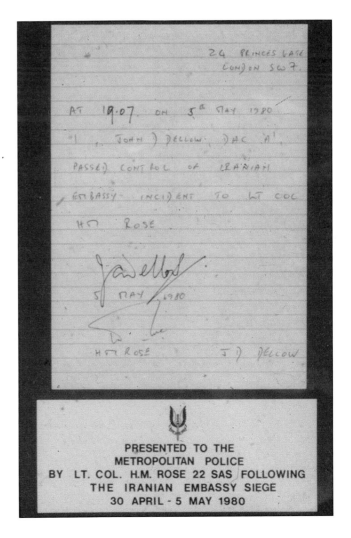

PRESENTED TO THE
METROPOLITAN POLICE
BY LT. COL. H.M. ROSE 22 SAS FOLLOWING
THE IRANIAN EMBASSY SIEGE
30 APRIL - 5 MAY 1980

*ABOVE: This hand-scribbled note authorised the SAS to take over from the Metropolitan Police at Princes Gate on 5 May 1980, after which Operation 'Nimrod' was activated.*

embassy and thought of clearing 50 rooms one by one, while all the time looking out for the terrorists and their prisoners.

### STORMING THE EMBASSY

'However, because the negotiators did their stuff, we were given a few days in which to prepare a more comprehensive plan, and we spent the time familiarising ourselves with every part of the building. The plan, like most good ones, was fairly simple: Red Team would enter and tackle the top half of the building, while Blue Team would clear the lower half of the embassy. We would also have the support of a multitude of snipers, which gave me, for one, a reassuring feeling.'

On the roof Red Team waited to undertake its part of the plan, which involved the use of two teams each of four men to abseil from the roof to the back balcony on the second storey of the building, a third team to assault the third storey, and a fourth team to blow in the skylight on the fourth storey so that its men could make their entry from the roof. Blue Team

was allocated the tasks of clearing the basement, ground and first storeys. Red Team began the operation, but then nearly destroyed its chances just as it was beginning:

'We were on the roof waiting for the order to go. We had all made our last-minute checks – respirators, weapons, assault suits and stun grenades – and now we wanted to be off. The adrenalin rush was unbelievable. The word was given and we started to descend from the roof. I fed the rope through my descender as we moved quickly and silently down the side of the rear of the building. Then, disaster. The boss got snagged in his harness. Some of the lads tried to help him, but then one of them accidentally broke a window with his foot.

'All hell broke loose as orders were screamed over the command net to storm the building. Snipers started firing CS gas into the embassy. We couldn't get the

## STUN GRENADE

One of the most effective items in the counter-terrorist armoury of the SAS Regiment, the stun grenade or 'flash-bang' was initially developed by the Regiment itself at Hereford. The 'weapon' is admirably suited to hostage-rescue operations as it is a small,

non-lethal device which contains magnesium powder and fulminate of mercury. After the ring has been pulled and the grenade thrown, the fulminate of mercury detonates with an extremely loud noise, and the detonation also ignites the magnesium to produce a temporarily blinding flash of up to 50,000 candlepower. The combination of the bang and flash produces an extreme level of physical and psychological disorientation among the unprotected for up to 45 seconds, giving the hostage-rescue team the opportunity to disable any terrorists. Stun grenades were used to great effect at Mogadishu and Princes Gate. Three examples of stun grenades currently available on the international market are the Condor SA GL-307, Royal Ordnance G60 and Haley and Weller E180.

boss free. Looking down I saw the lads from Blue Team using sledgehammers to break the glass and get in. The sound of gunfire filled the air as black-suited individuals started disappearing into the embassy. Jesus, what chaos!'

At the front of the building, on the first-storey balcony, a four-man SAS team placed a special frame charge against the glazing, but before this could be detonated the men had to yell at one of the hostages, BBC man Sim Harris, to move farther back into the embassy well away from the window. A few seconds later there was a loud explosion as the frame charge was detonated:

### STUNNING SUCCESS

'Then we were in. We threw in stun grenades and then quickly followed. There was a thundering bang and a blinding flash as the stun grenades went off. Designed to disorientate any hostiles who were in the room, they were a godsend. No one in here, good. I looked round, the stun grenades had set light to the curtains, not so good. No time to stop and put out the fire. Keep moving. We swept the room, then heard shouts

*BELOW: The attack is underway. Despite the speed of the SAS attack, the embassy quickly filled with smoke and flames – a result of CS grenades and the terrorists firing the building.*

coming from another office. We hurried towards the noise, and burst in to see one of the terrorists struggling with the copper who had been on duty when the embassy had been seized: PC Lock. One of the lads rushed forward and got Lock away, then pumped a long burst from his MP5 into the terrorist.

'Lock was bundled out and we continued our search. The building was filling with CS gas and smoke. We had to free the hostages and get out as quickly as possible. Where were they?'

## TERRORISING THE TERRORISTS

At first it had been imagined that the hostages were being held in an office at the rear of the building, and the men of Red Team expected to find them there as the troopers smashed the glass and hurled in stun grenades. These rooms were empty, however. The leader of the SAS operation was still tangled in his rope, and flames were now starting to lick his legs as inflammable material inside the Iranian Embassy building was ignited by the detonation of the stun grenades. Fortunately, one of the second wave of abseilers cut loose the commander, who crashed down

*ABOVE: The terrorists were quickly found and neutralised. Five of the six were killed inside the embassy, while the sixth managed to pass himself off as a hostage but was immediately captured.*

onto the balcony. One of the SAS soldiers smashed a window and hurled a stun grenade into a room containing a terrorist. The latter ran from the room and the SAS man raised his MP5 and pulled the trigger: the submachine gun jammed, and so the trooper drew his handgun and chased the terrorist, who ran to the embassy's Telex room. Here three other terrorists had just started to shoot at their hostages. The SAS troopers had to react swiftly and accurately:

'We heard the screams of the hostages coming from the telex room. "Shit, they're killing them all," I heard my mate shout. We raced into the room – pandemonium. There was a figure on the left with a grenade in his hand. One of the lads shot him with his Browning, a well aimed shot to the head which killed him instantly and blew his brains all over the place. We ordered everyone onto the floor. The terrorists had mixed themselves in with the hostages, and the latter were now going out of their heads. The women were screaming as we started to bundle them out of the room. One terrorist was identified, pulled out of the line and made to lie on the floor. Then he moved suspiciously and was shot – can't take any chances. His body was turned over; there was a Soviet hand grenade in his hand.

## CLEARING THE EMBASSY

'Another terrorist was shot trying to make his way down the stairs with the hostages. Keep moving. We forced our way into other rooms and began clearing them. Shoot off the lock, kick in the door, stun grenade, wait for the bang, then in and clear it. Empty. Keep going, and so it went on. By this time it was getting difficult to see, as the building was filling with smoke and the CS gas was working itself into every nook and cranny. I changed my magazine for a full one. Then we received the order across the command net – building clear, hostages safe. Time to leave. I was caked in sweat and my mouth was parched, but I felt elated because the operation had clearly been a success.'

The hostages and the one surviving terrorist were bound and secured on the lawn of the Iranian Embassy so that each one could be positively identified. Five of the terrorists had been killed inside the embassy:

'Salim' on the first-floor balcony, two in the Telex room, one in the hallway near the front door, and one in an office at the back of the building. Of the hostages, one had been killed and another injured by the terrorists during the course of the assault.

For the SAS, the whole operation was the clearest possible proof that its thinking and training concerning hostage-rescue operations was spot-on, but the aftermath was both good and bad for the SAS. Britain's most secret elite unit was suddenly a very public band of heroes. One of those who took part describes the result:

'Princes Gate was a turning point. It demonstrated to the powers that be what the Regiment could do and just what an asset the country had, but it also brought a problem we wished to avoid: the media spotlight. In addition, for the first few years after the siege, Selection courses were packed with what seemed like every man in the British Army wanting to join the SAS, and so we had to introduce extra physicals on the first day just to get rid of the wasters'.

*BELOW: The wrecked Iranian Embassy after the SAS rescue. The operation sent a clear message to hostage takers: you will not be tolerated and we have the means to defeat you.*

# CHAPTER 9

# EQUIPMENT

## Weapons are a key element in the capabilities of the SAS. Reliable, powerful and accurate, they must match the men's courage and determination for the operational task in hand.

### RIFLES

The most common weapon used by the SAS Regiment is the rifle in both its standard and assault forms, the latter being characterised by its ability to deliver full-automatic fire and, in its most modern incarnations, its overall design as a 'bullpup' weapon with a straight line through from the muzzle to the shoulder – a means on the one hand of reducing overall length and weight and on the other of increasing 'amiability' and accuracy in the automatic-fire mode.

*ABOVE: SAS soldiers photographed during jungle training. The weapon is a 5.56mm M16 assault rifle with M203 grenade launcher attached. This combination gives SAS four-man patrols good firepower.*

*LEFT: A modern Land Rover 110 vehicle. Used by the SAS, it has excellent power-to-weight ratio and can take a lot of punishment. SAS Land Rovers are usually armed to the teeth.*

### Heckler & Koch G3

This German weapon is an extremely reliable rifle that continues to function well under virtually all climatic and geographical conditions. This has made it attractive to a number of special forces around the world. The SAS has used it extensively in Northern Ireland.

**Calibre**: 7.62mm
**Weight**: 4.4kg (9.7lb) empty
**Length**: 1.025m (3ft 4.35in)
**Effective range** 400m (1305ft)
**Rate of fire:** 500-600 rounds per minute (cyclic)
**Feed**: 20-round box magazine
**Muzzle velocity** 780-800m (2559-2625ft) per second

### Heckler & Koch G41

This is essentially the G3 revised to fire 5.56mm ammunition. Other changes include provision for a fixed or retractable butt, a 30-round magazine and a three-round

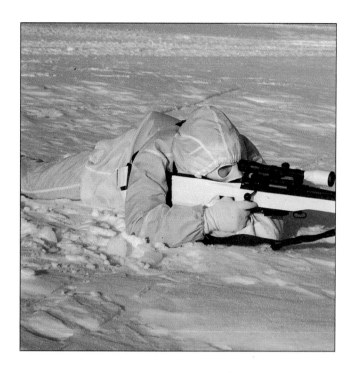

*ABOVE: The SAS's current sniper rifle, the 7.62mm Accuracy International PM. This bolt-action, precision-made, 10-round rifle is accurate to a range of 1000m (3285ft).*

burst capability. The type is made the more attractive to special forces, including the SAS, by its low noise signature and its dustproof ejector port.

**Calibre:** 5.56mm
**Weight:** 4.1kg (9.04lb) empty with fixed butt or 4.35kg (9.59lb) empty with retractable butt
**Length:** 0.997m (3ft 3.25in) with fixed butt or 0.806m (2 ft 7.75in) with retractable butt retracted
**Effective range:** 400m (1305ft)
**Rate of fire:** 850 rounds per minute (cyclic)
**Feed:** 30-round box magazine
**Muzzle velocity:** 800m (2625ft) per second

### Colt M16

This is one of the world's most widely used assault rifles. A product of the US Army's search for a light, sturdy, accurate weapon which fired 7.62mm NATO standard ammunition in the 1950s, the M16 entered service in 1959.

Experience in Southeast Asia soon convinced the US Army that the M16 was not self-cleaning and daily maintenance of the gas passages was required. In addition, a thumb-operated plunger was needed on the right of the receiver to ensure that the bolt was fully closed in muddy conditions. These changes turned the M16 into the M16A1, an increasingly ubiquitous weapon. The current version is the M16A2.

The SAS felt that the M16A1 was ideal for its purposes in jungle fighting, and so adopted the weapon for the campaign in Borneo (1963-66). The weapon was then used in Aden, Oman and later in the Falklands and Gulf Wars. The M16A2 used by the SAS can fire three-round bursts as well as single shots, but lacks the capacity for full-automatic fire found in some export versions of the M16 series.

**Calibre:** 5.56mm
**Weight:** 3.4kg (7.5lb) empty
**Length:** 1.0m (3ft 3.4in)
**Effective range:** 400m (1305ft)
**Rate of fire:** 700-900 rounds per minute (cyclic)
**Feed:** 20- or 30-round detachable box magazine
**Muzzle velocity:** 991m (3250ft) per second with the M193 round or 948m (3110ft) per second with the SS109 round

### SNIPER RIFLES

The SAS uses the sniper rifle for two different and highly contrasting roles. The first is in 'conventional' warfare, where a sniper must be capable of scoring a first-round hit (but not necessarily a kill) on a head-sized target at a range of 300m (990ft) or a torso-sized target at a range of between 600 and 1000m (1965 and 3285ft). The second is for use in counter-revolutionary and hostage-rescue operations, when a first-round kill rather than hit at a range that may be as short as 100m (328ft) is critical.

### L96A1

The 7.62mm Accuracy International PM replaced the L42 used until 1982 (including the Falklands War). It entered SAS service as the L96A1 bolt-action rifle; it has a plastic stock, a light bipod under the barrel and a monopod under the stock so that the rifle can be laid on the target for long periods without tiring the firer. Schmidt & Bender telescopic sights provide accuracy of fire to a range of 1000m (3285ft).

**Calibre:** 7.62mm
**Weight:** 6.5kg (14.3lb) empty
**Length:** 1.124-1.194m (3ft 4.25in to 3ft 11in)
**Effective range:** 1000m (3285ft)
**Feed:** 10-round box magazine
**Muzzle velocity:** 914m (3000ft) per second

### SHOTGUNS

The SAS first used shotguns in action during the Malayan 'Emergency' (1948-60), initially employing the Browning auto-loader. This civilian weapon

worked well under jungle conditions and proved effective in close combat. The SAS now uses the shotgun for counter-terrorist operations, principally for blowing off door hinges at the moment an assault team moves into a room. Modern military shotguns are optimised for this type of job as they can fire a number of different cartridges, among them buckshot, armour-piercing, CS gas, and Hatton (hinge-removing) and others.

### Remington 870
**Calibre:** 12 gauge
**Weight:** 3.6kg (7.94lb) empty
**Length:** 1.06m (3ft 5.75in)
**Effective range:** 40m (1312ft)
**Feed:** seven-round internal magazine
**Muzzle velocity:** dependant on the type of round used

*ABOVE: Used by the SAS since the 1970s, the MP5 submachine gun fires from a closed bolt. This means that when the trigger is pulled the bolt does not slam forward and disturb the aim.*

*LEFT: The Regiment's favoured handgun, the 9mm Browning High Power. Despite being 60 years old, it has a large magazine capacity, semi-automatic action and good stopping power.*

## HANDGUNS

The SAS Regiment has used the pistol or handgun since its earliest days, but this use has been in two widely different roles. In World War II, the handgun was used in its standard role as a side arm for personal protection, but in more recent years it has become a weapon associated with counter-terrorist operations. There has been considerable argument about the relative merits of the submachine gun and handgun for this role, some arguing that the submachine gun offers greater capability through its higher weight of fire and single-shot accuracy, but others pointing out the advantages of the handgun for its rapid-fire capability at ranges up to 30m (99ft), easy 'pointability', and more effective single-handed use. Critics of the handgun also aver that the pistol has so high a recoil force that any second shot is generally less accurate than the first, but the SAS has circumvented this problem by specialised training.

### Browning High Power
In the period after World War II, the SAS used a number of American and European handguns, most notably the American-designed Colt M1911A1 and Browning High Power, and the European-designed Glock and SIG Sauer weapons. The Browning High Power, made in Belgium by Fabrique Nationale has become synonymous with the SAS. The weapon has a semi-automatic action, considerable stopping power and a large magazine. The High Power has been produced and used in a number of forms, but the current model is the BDA (Browning Double Action), in which the hammer can be cocked manually before the trigger is pulled to fire the weapon, or alternatively the hammer can be cocked and the weapon fired by continuous pressure on the trigger.
**Calibre:** 9mm
**Weight:** 0.905kg (2lb) empty
**Length:** 0.2m (7.9in)
**Effective range:** 40m (132ft)
**Feed:** 14-round box magazine
**Muzzle velocity:** 253m (830ft) per second

## SUBMACHINE GUNS

The submachine gun is a pistol-calibre weapon designed to deliver selective or automatic fire, and is

Heckler & Koch MP5 series, which is available in a number of forms that are all excellent weapons (within the limitations already described for the submachine gun) of typically good German design and manufacture for safety and reliability. The baseline weapon is the MP5, which has the advantage of firing from a closed-bolt position: when the trigger is pulled, the bolt is already in the forward position against the breech, meaning that activation of the trigger merely releases the firing pin to fire the already chambered cartridge, resulting in no forward movement of the gun's centre of mass and thus no disturbance of aim. The main variants of the MP5 are the MP5A2, with a fixed plastic butt, and the MP5A3, with a sliding butt that can be extended or retracted on a single strut. A derivative much favoured by the SAS for use in Northern Ireland, as it can be operated as a submachine gun or as an assault rifle, is the Heckler & Koch HK53, which is in essence a derivative of the MP5 revised for the 5.56mm round.

**Calibre:** 9mm

**Weight:** 2.55kg (5.62lb) empty

**Length:** 0.68m (2ft 2.75in) for the MP5A2 and 0.66m (2ft 2in) for the MP5A3 with the but extended, or 0.49m (1ft 7.3in) for the MP5A3 with the stock retracted

**Effective range:** 200m (660ft)

**Rate of fire:** 800 rounds per minute (cyclic)

**Feed:** 15- or 30-round box magazine

**Muzzle velocity:** 400m (1312ft) per second

*ABOVE: The General Purpose Machine Gun (GPMG) has served the SAS all over the world, from the freezing wastes of South Georgia to the heat of Iraq. Its 7.62mm round has excellent range.*

generally associated with close-range combat and a firing position at the shoulder or the waist. Generally replaced after World War II by the assault rifle, the submachine gun's popularity revived during the 1960s. Such weapons are characterised by a short effective range and a very high rate of fire (typically 800-1000 rounds per minute to ensure the killing of a terrorist by one burst of fire). The magazine can be emptied very rapidly, however. Another problem is that the submachine gun almost invariably fires from an open-bolt position, which means the movement of the reciprocating parts makes accurate fire almost impossible.

### Heckler & Koch MP5

The primary submachine used by the SAS is the

## MACHINE GUNS

Despite its high rate of ammunition consumption, which is always a problem for foot patrols with their limited weight-carrying capabilities, the machine gun has always played a prominent part in SAS operations. In the hands of a well trained trooper it can offset many aspects of an enemy's numerical superiority. It is a vital fire-support weapon: the light machine gun provides support for the squad and covers troopers as they advance, the medium machine gun lays down sustained fire in an area in which enemy movement is thus impossible, and the heavy machine gun provides multiple capabilities in offensive and defensive operations. It is a weapon vital to the typical four-man SAS in all types of operation.

### L7A2 General Purpose Machine Gun

From the late 1950s, the survivors of the older machine guns operated by the SAS were supplemented and then supplanted by the 7.62mm General Purpose Machine Gun (GPMG), which is the medium machine gun counterpart of the L1 semi-automatic rifle and designated L7 in British Army service. The GPMG is extremely reliable and is notable for its accuracy, especially in the delivery of short bursts that can be so effective in engagements of the type so common to the SAS. The weapon is generally used on a bipod, but can be installed on a tripod for the sustained-fire role.

**Calibre:** 7.62mm
**Weight:** 10.9kg (24lb) with a bipod
**Length:** 1.232m (4ft 0.5in) in the light role or 1.048m (3ft 5.25in) in the sustained role
**Effective range:** 1805m (5925ft)
**Rate of fire:** 750-1000 rounds per minute (cyclic)
**Feed:** belt
**Muzzle velocity:** 838m (2750ft) per second

### Minimi

Used by the SAS in the 1991 Gulf War, this light, compact 5.56mm machine gun is ideal for foot patrols. Well made, accurate and able to take M16 magazines via one of its two feed slots, it will become increasingly important to SAS patrols in the future.

**Calibre:** 5.56mm
**Weight:** 6.8kg (15lb)
**Length:** 1.04m (41in)
**Effective range:** 600m (1968ft)
**Rate of fire:** 750-1000 rounds per minute (cyclic)
**Feed:** 30-round box magazine or 200-round metal belt
**Muzzle velocity:** 915m (3000ft) per second

## SUPPORT WEAPONS

As a unit designed for operations deep in the enemy's rear areas, the SAS cannot rely on support from the heavier weapons of associated units and, as it is optimised for speed and agility to minimise the chances of interception by heavier enemy forces, its patrols mostly always operate in the lightest possible condition and therefore cannot possess organic heavy support weapons such as heavy mortars and/or field artillery.

The SAS is intended primarily to provide a reconnaissance and intelligence-gathering capability. Its members should therefore avoid major engagements with the enemy, but they are inevitably required to stand and fight on occasion. For this reason, therefore, they require support weapons of some lighter types to increase the chances of survival. The mortar is traditionally associated with the provision of close fire sup-port for infantry units up to the battalion in size. Such fire support can also be provided by field artillery, but the availability of the mortar as an organic element of the infantry unit offers greater flexibility and a faster response time. The SAS generally operates far beyond the support capability of friendly artillery, so the mortar has become and will continue to be the cornerstone of the SAS's support capability in both offensive and defensive operations.

### L16A1

The Regiment's current mortar is the Mortar, ML, 81mm, otherwise known as the L16. This is an advanced weapon capable of delivering its bombs accurately over a long range as a result of its nicely engineered barrel and the use of a plastic sealing ring to trap the propellant gases behind the bomb with minimum leakage.

**Calibre:** 81mm (3.19in)
**Weight:** 34.6kg (76.28lb)
**Maximum range:** 5650m (18,540ft)
**Bomb weight:** 4.26kg (9.39lb) for the HE round

### Carl Gustav

The anti-tank weapon most generally associated with the SAS since the later 1950s has been a Swedish model, the Carl Gustav M2-550 recoilless gun. This is sturdy, reliable, accurate and versatile, the last factor being generated by the Carl Gustav's ability to fire an anti-personnel round as well as an anti-tank round. Some indication of the weapon's tactical flexibility is provided by the fact that during the Falklands War (1982), a Royal Marine used his Carl Gustav first to

ABOVE: *The 5.56mm Minimi is becoming increasingly popular with SAS patrols. Light and accurate, it can fire M16 rounds, which means patrols can standardise on ammunition.*

shoot down an Argentine helicopter, and then to put a hole though the side plate of an Argentine destroyer.

**Calibre:** 84mm (3.31in)
**Weight:** 15kg (33.1lb)
**Length:** 1.13m (3ft 8.5in)
**Round weight:** 3kg (6.61lb) for the hollow-charge projectile
**Muzzle velocity:** 380m (1247ft) per second
**Maximum range:** 1000m (3285ft)
**Armour penetration:** 400mm (15.75in) at any range

During the 1960s there were many who felt that a reloadable weapon such as the Carl Gustav was unnecessarily complex, too heavy and also too expensive, and as a result many countries developed single-shot anti-armour weapons. Once the launcher had been fired the empty tube was discarded, and the operator then picked up a fresh unit, delivered as a certified round ready for battlefield use. The weapon of this type used by the SAS is the American M72.

### M72A2

Accurate and fitted with a potent warhead, the M72 is light enough that several complete units can be carried by a single man. Its main disadvantage, shared by many weapons of the same type, is a prominent firing signature. This requires a rapid departure of the operator after he has discharged the weapon and discarded the spent launch tube to avoid enemy fire.

**Calibre:** 66mm (2.6in)
**Weight:** 2.36kg (5.2lb)
**Length:** 0.655m (2ft 1.8in) closed or 0.893m (2ft 11.15in) extended for firing
**Rocket weight:** 1kg (2.2lb)

*ABOVE: The one-shot, throwaway M72 anti-tank weapon. Capable of knocking out most modern main battle tanks, it weighs only 2.36kg (5.2lb), making it ideal for SAS operations.*

**Muzzle velocity:** 145m (475ft) per second
**Maximum range:** 1000m (3285ft)
**Armour penetration:** 305mm (12in) at any range

The most important current anti-aircraft weapons for the use of ground forces is the surface-to-air missile, and the particular type generally issued to infantry units is the shoulder-launched surface-to-air missile (SAM), which generally comprises a comparatively small missile (with solid-propellant rocket propulsion and an infrared guidance package) carried in a disposable sealed container/launcher tube that is clipped to a reusable sight and trigger unit in use. In general, however, SAS patrols are not equipped with such weapons for three reasons. First, SAS patrols rarely operate from static bases that require defence against fixed- and rotary-wing warplanes: even when such a base is used, the practice of the SAS is to make this base so well camouflaged that it is effectively invisible to warplanes. Second, SAS patrols carrying even lightweight shoulder-launched SAMs would find their ability to move rapidly severely compromised. Third, the SAS's fieldcraft and camouflage skills make the use of shoulder-launched SAMs generally superfluous in mobile operations.

There are limited occasions (notably arctic and desert warfare operations) in which shoulder-launched SAMs are useful, however, and for this eventuality the SAS currently has a shoulder-launched SAM of Western origins.

### FIM-92A1 Stinger

This was designed as a successor to the General Dynamic's first-generation, and therefore highly limited, Redeye shoulder-launched SAM. Stinger has an all-aspect engagement capability, greater performance and manoeuvrability, an IFF system and enhanced resistance to electronic countermeasures. The weapon was introduced in 1981 and has proved generally successful with its passive infrared homing system. The missile and launcher weigh 13.6kg (30lb), or 15.1kg (33.3lb) with the IFF system and battery.

**Diameter:** 0.07m (2.75in)
**Length:** 1.52m (5ft 0in)
**Weight:** 10.1kg (22.3lb)
**Warhead:** 3kg (6.6lb) proximity-fused blast/fragmentation
**Maximum speed:** more than Mach 2
**Maximum range:** 5030m (16,500ft)

ABOVE: *The famous SAS 'Pink Panther' Land Rover. In SAS service in the 1960s, the colour scheme was designed to make it blend into the pink haze often encountered in desert terrain.*

## VEHICLES

The SAS is essentially an infantry unit, but from its very beginnings was designed for delivery into its operational area by land, sea or air, and there to operate on foot or, wherever possible, light vehicles to increase the speed, scope and flexibility of its activities and thereby increase its overall efficiency in the reconnaissance and/or sabotage roles.

### Land Rover Defender 110

The vehicle most famously associated with the SAS is currently the Land Rover, which replaced the Jeep of World War II during the 1950s. It is an eloquent testimony to the overall capabilities of the Land Rover, especially in terms of payload-carrying capability and reliability, that the SAS can choose from any such vehicle in the world but has opted for so long for the British-made Land Rover series.

Since 1984 production has been of the Land Rover 90 and Land Rover 110 series with short and long wheelbases respectively, and these are the current mainstays of the Land Rover force in service with the British forces, which also uses the stretched Land Rover 130 as an ambulance and artillery tractor. Shortly before the Iraqi invasion of Kuwait in August 1990, which sparked the UN response that culminated in the 'Desert Storm' campaign of January/February 1991, Land Rover renamed its military vehicles in the Defender series, which is the designation currently in use during the mid-1990s.

The SAS mostly uses the long-wheelbase variant because of its greater payload-carrying capability. The most famous variant is the 'Pink Panther', which has served faithfully as the Regiment's long-range desert patrol vehicle. Operated since the early 1960s, the 'Pink Panther' is basically a version of the long-wheelbase Land Rover Series II with a spare wheel mounted over the front bumper, no doors, smoke canisters, and an overall pink colour scheme designed to make the vehicles blend into the typically pink haze often encountered in desert conditions.

The SAS currently uses a modest number of short-wheelbase Land Rover Defender 90 vehicles with the nickname 'Dinky', and a considerably larger number of long-wheelbase Land Rover Defender 110 vehicles. The latter offer a better ride, greater stopping power and an improved turning circle than their predecessors as a result of the incorporation of the type of coil-spring suspension pioneered by the Range Rover civilian vehicle, front-wheel disc brakes and revision of the steering system.

**Weight:** 3050kg (6725lb)

**Dimensions:** length 4.669m (15ft 4in); width 1.79m (5ft 10.5in); height 2.035m (6ft 8in)

**Payload:** driver, and up to eight passengers or freight

**Engine:** one Rover 3.528-litre petrol engine delivering 95.4kw (128hp) to four wheels

**Fuel capacity:** 79.5 litres (17.5Imp gal)

**Performance:** speed 121km/h (75mph); range 748km (465 miles); ground clearance 0.216m (8.5in)

ABOVE: *The American Stinger surface-to-air missile (SAM) gives SAS vehicle and foot patrols effective and manportable anti-aircraft defence. It was first used by the Regiment in the Falklands.*

# INDEX